The Psalms

Prayers for the
Ups, Downs and In-Betweens
of Life

A Literary-Experiential Approach

Background Books 2

The Psalms

Prayers for the
Ups, Downs and In-Betweens
of Life

A Literary-Experiential Approach

John F. Craghan

 Michael Glazier, Inc.

Wilmington, Delaware

About the Author

John F. Craghan did his graduate studies at the University of Munich, the Pontifical Biblical Institute and Columbia University. He is presently teaching at the University of Wisconsin at Oshkosh. His publications include *Love and Thunder: A Spirituality of the Old Testament* and *Esther, Judith, Tobit, Jonah, Ruth*, Volume 16 of the Old Testament Message series. He is an associate editor of the *Biblical Theology Bulletin*.

First published in 1985 by Michael Glazier, Inc., 1723 Delaware Avenue, Wilmington, Delaware 19806 • ©1985 by John F. Craghan. All rights reserved. • Library of Congress Card Catalog Number: 84-81245 • International Standard Book Number: 0-89453-439-4 • Printed in the United States of America.

Contents

For
My Mother,
Margaret Shannon Craghan,
A Woman of Deep Prayer,
On the Occasion of
Her 80th Birthday

Preface

This book is an outgrowth of courses on the Psalms that I gave at the Theological Institute of St. Norbert College, De Pere, Wisconsin; the Graduate School of Education of Fairfield University, Fairfield, Connecticut; and the Graduate School of Religion and Religious Education of Fordham University, Bronx, New York. On these occasions I have observed a renewed interest in the Psalms, especially from the vantage point of prayer and spirituality. This book then is a modest effort to respond to such interest. It attempts to suggest ways in which the Psalms can nourish private prayer (although there is no such category as purely private prayer). It also seeks to recommend ways in which the Psalms can enrich communal prayer in the recitation of the Liturgy of the Hours, preparation for Eucharist, paraliturgical services, etc. At all costs it underlines the interaction of God, the community, and the individual in the act of prayer.

While I have arranged the Psalms according to their different literary types (e. g., hymns, laments, royal psalms), I have also followed the insight of W. Brueggemann, viz., that these different types correspond to various cycles in our life of faith. At the same time I have used the literary approach of L. Alonso Schökel, emphasizing symbol, imagery, structure, and movement. It will be all too apparent how much I am indebted to the work of these two scholars.

In adapting modern biblical advances to the needs of a wider audience, I have chosen to relegate certain materials to the notes for those who are interested in pursuing particular points. The Psalter, however, is not the private treasure of the scholar but the patrimony of the believing community. Moreover, for the Christian community the New Testament shows how the prayer book of Israel may be appropriated in a fresh way.

For the biblical text I have used the Revised Standard Version (RSV) along with its enumeration and versification of the Psalms. In general I have left the text as it is. Only on occasion do I suggest textual changes, and then solely in the interests of clarity. In keeping with the translation I have employed masculine pronouns and pronominal adjectives in speaking of God. However, this by no means implies that God and the human community are exclusively male. Indeed both the masculine and the feminine imagery of God ultimately envisions genuine covenant partners who seek to become ever more human.

Finally I have the pleasant task of expressing my thanks to two people who have contributed significantly to the making of this book. I am grateful to my wife Barbara for her encouragement and help during the entire process of composition. As the dedication indicates, I am particularly grateful to my mother. In her fervent way of praying the rosary she taught me how to approach and appreciate the Psalms. This book, therefore, is a small gesture of my great indebtedness to her.

John F. Craghan
Green Bay, Wisconsin

Abbreviations

BOOKS OF THE BIBLE

1 Cor	First Corinthians	Mic	Micah
Deut	Deuteronomy	Mk	Mark
Eccl	Ecclesiastes	Num	Numbers
Ex	Exodus	1 Pet	First Peter
Ezek	Ezekiel	Prov	Proverbs
Heb	Hebrews	Ps (s)	Psalm(s)
Hos	Hosea	Rom	Romans
Isa	Isaiah	1 Sam	First Samuel
Jer	Jeremiah	2 Sam	Second Samuel
Matt	Matthew	Wis	Wisdom

JOURNALS, SERIES, ETC.

AB	Anchor Bible
BASOR	Bulletin of the American Schools of Oriental Research
BK	Bibel und Kirche
BKAT	Biblischer Kommentar: Altes Testament
BTB	Biblical Theology Bulletin
CBQ	Catholic Biblical Quarterly
CTM	Concordia Theological Monthly

IDBSup	Supplementary volume to *Interpreter's Dictionary of the Bible*
Int	*Interpretation*
JAAR	*Journal of the American Academy of Religion*
JBC	*Jerome Biblical Commentary*
JBL	*Journal of Biblical Literature*
JSOT	*Journal for the Study of the Old Testament*
TB	*Tyndale Bulletin*
TDNT	*Theological Dictionary of the New Testament*
TDOT	*Theological Dictionary of the Old Testament*
TS	*Theological Studies*
VT	*Vetus Testamentum*
VTSup	Supplements to *Vetus Testamentum*
ZAW	*Zeitschrift für die alttestamentliche Wissenschaft*

1

Prayer, Psalms, Movement

What is the nature of prayer? What kind of of prayer are the Psalms? Can the Psalms reflect the movements in our lives with their ups, downs, and in-betweens? It is the purpose of this opening chapter to attempt at least partial answers to these ever valid questions.

The nature of prayer[1]

Prayer is as urgent a pastoral problem as ever. While we are the beneficiaries, we are also the victims of the computer age. We are served up instant information, much of it discouraging, and challenged to swallow the main course and even ask for dessert. Our television newscasters package much of this information, blocking out some items and seasoning the remains with their own view of things. Our church communities also assess the world, national, and local events, seeking to uncover God's viewpoint and suggesting the proper way of responding. Prayer and the computer age may strike us as being odd bedfellows. But the fact is that they cannot be separated.

[1]In developing this section I am very much indebted to my teacher and colleague, Rev. Eugene A. McAlee, C.SS.R., for his perception and advice.

St. Alphonsus de Liguori, the Doctor of Prayer, called prayer the great means of salvation.[2] Although his eighteenth century world was quite different from ours, his teaching on prayer is as timely as ever. Prayer, both individual and communal, must reply to this information saturation with faith, hope, and charity. Being grounded in the Holy One of Israel,[3] we must dare to expect a new world by reacting to the needs of others which are ultimately the needs of our God. Prayer is not a cop-out from the facts of life, not a retreat to never-never land where pain is lulled and anxiety is sedated.[4] Prayer is the negation of passive observers and non-participants. Prayer is the affirmation of the totally involved. We have to respond to our world in either belief or disbelief. We stand at the crossroads and are challenged to decide. The decision is: to pray or not to pray.

What does prayer do for us? It forces us to interiorize and reflect. It urges us to dismiss the party line and search ever more deeply into the real, the shocking meaning of daily events. Prayer leads us to adopt different stances, depending on the nature of our world and our own predicament. It can express itself in awe and wonder. It can loosen the gravitational pull of our ego to focus on the goodness of our God, of fellow humans, of that joint divine-human venture we call love. It can express itself in thanksgiving. It can lead us to acknowledge the radical newness in our lives which clamors to be known in the song of praise. Prayer can express itself

---

[2] St. Alphonsus de Liguori, *The Great Means of Salvation and Perfection* (New York: Benziger, 1886) 23-49.

[3] For the significance of this phrase in First Isaiah see T. C. Vriezen, "Essentials of the Theology of Isaiah," *Israel's Prophetic Heritage: Essays in Honor of James Muilenburg* (ed. B. W. Anderson & W. Harrelson; New York: Harper, 1962) 131-134. For the centrality of this phrase in the Book of Isaiah see W. L. Holladay, *Isaiah: Scroll of a Prophetic Heritage* (Grand Rapids: Eerdmans, 1978) 17-19. For the liturgical influence in the Isaiah tradition see J. Eaton, "The Isaiah Tradition," *Israel's Prophetic Heritage: Essays in Honour of Peter R. Ackroyd* (ed. R. Coggins et al.; Cambridge: Cambridge University, 1982) 58-76.

[4] A. Heschel (*Man's Quest for God: Studies in Prayer and Symbolism* [New York: Scribner, 1954] .7) writes: "We do not step out of the world when we pray; we merely see the world in a different setting."

in pain and frustration. It can awaken us to our personal problems and the problems of others. Prayer reminds us that we must share these problems in order to be redeemed.

Prayer allows us to think the thoughts of God, not of humans. As A. Heschel put it so well, "The purpose of language is to inform; the purpose of prayer is to partake."[5] Through prayer we become conformed to the image of God's Son who felt the compulsion for seasons of prayer, who was Luke's paragon of prayer,[6] and who prayed Israel's Psalms in a new key. The trajectory of prayer is to become selfless, not selfish, to become transfigured, not disfigured. Prayer constrains us to ask "what is your will?" not "what is the administration's policy?" Prayer is admission into the frightening world where slogans limp and clichés self-destruct. To pray is to acknowledge that things can be otherwise and that we do make a difference.

Prayer allows us to brush up against God himself. We are ushered into the presence of One who does not insist on churchy language, who permits, indeed encourages us to employ the raw language of pain and the bubbly vocabulary of joy. Prayer means that God can touch our psyche, piercing to the division of joints and marrow (see Heb 4:12). Prayer is not the privilege of the select few, but the absolute necessity of all.[7] Not to brush up against this God is to cease to be in contact with reality. At prayer we are truly our-

[5] *Ibid.*, 16.

[6] For the significance of prayer in Luke see L. O. Harris, "Prayer in the Gospel of Luke," *Southwestern Journal of Theology* 10 (1967) 59-69; J. Navone, *Themes of St. Luke* (Rome: Gregorian University, 1970) 118-131; H. H. Conn, "Luke's Theology of Prayer," *Christianity Today* 17 (1972-73) 6-8 (290-292); P. T. O'Brien, "Prayer in Luke-Acts," *TB* 24 (1973) 111-127; A. A. Trites, "The Prayer Motif in Luke-Acts," *Perspectives on Luke-Acts* (ed. C. H. Talbert; Danville, Virginia: Association of Baptist Professors of Religion, 1978) 168-186.
Baptist Professors of Religion, 1978) 168-186.

[7] See St. Alphonsus de Liguori, *The Great Means*, 28. A. Heschel (*Man's Quest*, 78) is strikingly similar: "Prayer is not a need but *an ontological necessity* (author's italics), an act that constitutes the very essence of man. He who has never prayed is not fully human."

selves: weeping and rejoicing, praising and cursing, hearing and being heard.

Prayer empowers us to interact with our computer world. At prayer we find the courage to challenge our world where the temptation always lurks to treat people as things. At prayer we discover the means to listen to the pain of others and offer healing. At prayer we experience the goodness of others and the encouragement to make that goodness known to a larger audience. At prayer we celebrate the reliability of our God and hence derive confidence to undertake new ventures.

The Psalms

The Psalms[8] (derived from a Greek word meaning a song sung to the accompaniment of a harplike instrument) are prayer. Although it is virtually impossible to pinpoint the authors of these prayers and their original setting, they remain the prayer book of Israel. They are the distillation of her encounter with Yahweh,[9] other nations, and herself over many centuries. They express in prayer form the successes and failures of Israel. Actually the general anonymity of the writers and their original setting is a plus.[10] Instead of being unique, once and for all expressions, the Psalms have become Israel's typical experience of prayer.

[8] For more extensive introductions to the Psalms see A. Weiser, *The Psalms: A Commentary* (Old Testament Library; Philadelphia: Westminster, 1962) 19-101; C. Barth, *Introduction to the Psalms* (New York: Scribner, 1966); B. W. Anderson, *Out of the Depths: The Psalms Speak for Us Today* (Philadelphia: Westminster, 1970) 1-21; L. Sabourin, *The Psalms: Their Origin and Meaning* (New York: Alba House, 1974) 3-62; R. E. Murphy, *The Psalms, Job* (Proclamation Commentaries; Philadelphia: Fortress, 1977) 15-46; C. Stuhlmueller, *Psalms* (Old Testament Message; Wilmington: Michael Glazier, 1983), 1. 15-55.

[9] Although the RSV consistently translates the personal name of the God of Israel as "Lord," "Yahweh" is the preferred rendering here apart from actual citations of the biblical text.

[10] For the interaction of author and community with the subsequent loss of the author's personality see L. Alonso Schökel, *The Inspired Word: Scripture in the Light of Language and Literature* (New York: Herder & Herder, 1965) 229-230.

The Psalms are also our prayers.[11] The fact that they are included in the canon of Sacred Scripture indicates that there is a certain commonality between Israel's experience and our own. This involves the task of hermeneutics, i.e., the science of determining how (in this instance) the prayers in Israel's cultural context may be understood in our own.[12] Actually the utter humanity of the Psalms simplifies this process. As prayers, the Psalms deal in typical fashion with basic human problems and situations.[13] They employ common symbols, such as water, light, and space, which are transcultural. The prayer of the temple and the synagogue is thereby the prayer of the church as well.[14] The history of

[11] Authors who have sought to relate the Psalms to New Testament theology include the following: S. Terrien, *The Psalms and Their Meaning for Today* (New York: Bobbs-Merrill, 1952); R. B. Y. Scott, *The Psalms as Christian Prayer* (World Christian Books; New York: Association Press, 1958); T. Worden, *The Psalms Are Christian Prayer* (London: Chapman, 1962); A. Gelin, *The Psalms Are Our Prayers* (Collegeville, Minnesota: The Liturgical Press, 1963); A. George, *Praying the Psalms: A Guide for Using the Psalms as Christian Prayer* (Notre Dame: Fides, 1964); P. Drijvers, *The Psalms: Their Structure and Meaning* (New York: Herder & Herder, 1965); C. Barth, *Introduction to the Psalms*; H. H. Guthrie, *Israel's Sacred Songs: A Study of Dominant Themes* (New York: Seabury, 1966); B. W. Anderson, *Out of the Depths*; L. Alonso Schökel, *Treinta Salmos: Poesía y oración* (Estudios de Antiguo Testamento 2; Madrid: Christiandad, 1981).

[12] For the roles of canon and hermeneutics see the following: B. S. Childs, "The Old Testament as Scripture of the Church," *CTM* 43 (1972) 709-722; "Reflections on the Modern Study of the Psalms," *Magnalia Dei. The Mighty Acts of God: In Memoriam George Ernest Wright* (ed. F. M. Cross et al.; Garden City, New York: Doubleday, 1976) 377-388; *Introduction to the Old Testament as Scripture* (Philadelphia: Fortress, 1979) 504-525; J. A. Sanders, *Torah and Canon* (2d ed.; Philadelphia: Fortress, 1974); "Adaptable for Life: The Nature and Function of Canon," *Magnalia Dei*, 531-560; "Hermeneutics," *IDBSup*, 402-407; S. M. Schneiders, "Faith, Hermeneutics, and the Literal Sense of Scripture," *TS* 39 (1978) 719-736; "The Paschal Imagination: Objectivity and Subjectivity in New Testament Interpretation," *TS* 43 (1982) 52-68.

[13] See H. Ringgren, *The Faith of the Psalmists* (Philadelphia: Fortress, 1963) 114.

[14] For a concise statement of the use of the Psalms in Christian tradition see M. H. Shepherd, *The Psalms in Christian Worship: A Practical Guide* (Collegeville, Minnesota: The Liturgical Press, 1976). For a sensitive approach to the Christian appropriation of Jewish psalms see W. Brueggemann, *Praying the Psalms* (Winona, Minnesota: Saint Mary's, 1982) 51-64.

Israel thus coalesces with the history of the church and our own personal history.

The basis of Israel's prayer — and our prayer as well — is the covenant. Covenant may be described as a relationship in which a moral connection between parties is defined and affirmed.[15] However, this relationship is never one-on-one but always triangular: Yahweh, the community, and the individual Israelite. Covenant and hence prayer based on covenant is always a dangerous undertaking. It presumes that the individual can truly interact with God only by including the community. Even the most personal and intimate prayer of an individual is bound up with the good of the community. We truly honor this God by looking to the needs of this God's community. Prayer rooted in covenant exposes the shallowness of the following statement: "God never gets in my way, only humans do!"

The Psalms are cultic prayer. According to the insight of S. Mowinckel the Psalms have their setting in community worship where the "I" of the psalmist corresponds to the "we" of the community.[16] They are not the random compositions of individual gifted poets but the works of Israel's great littérateurs that have become the patrimony of the worshipping community. In general, therefore, the Psalms were written for use in Israel's liturgy. This insight, far from denigrating personal prayer, reveals that such prayer must always have community contours.[17] Purely egocentric prayer is a caricature of prayer.

[15] See J. F. Craghan, *Love and Thunder: A Spirituality of the Old Testament* (Collegeville, Minnesota: The Liturgical Press, 1983) 29-39 for the pertinent literature on covenant.

[16] S. Mowinckel, *The Psalms in Israel's Worship* (New York: Abingdon, 1962), 2. 1-25,31-43. In discussing Psalm 90, G. von Rad (*God at Work in Israel* [Nashville: Abingdon, 1980] 211) expresses this perception in these terms: "His intention is not at all to express what only he could express in that way and no other has yet expressed. On the contrary, he includes the others also in his 'I'; through him there speaks not only the isolated individual, but rather mankind on a much more inclusive basis than that of a single individual."

[17] See H. Ringgren, *The Faith of the Psalmists* 20-26. R. Albertz has examined the tension between public and familial piety, noting that the royal, priestly

The Psalms are poetry, not prose. The chief characteristic of Hebrew poetry is parallelism or a rhythm of sense. In synonymous parallelism the second part or stich echoes the first in slightly different language. For example, Ps 2:1:

> Why do the nations conspire and the peoples plot in vain?

In antithetic parallelism the second part or stich opposes the first. For example, Ps 1:6:

> For the Lord knows the way of the righteous, but the way of the wicked will perish.

In synthetic parallelism the second part or stich develops or complements the first. For example, Ps 95:3:

> For the Lord is a great God, and a great King above all gods.

In appropriating this poetry for our own prayer,[18] we immediately note that it may jar our regular prayer formulas. In many ways the theological language of the west is cerebral and conceptual. We feel more at home with dogmatic definitions or third person statements about this God. We tend to prefer "The Omnipotent One in his divine providence will not permit his creation to miscarry" to "The Lord is my shepherd, I shall not want" (Ps 23:1). We are likely to choose "To the Godhead latria or worship is due" over:

establishment in Israel did not subsume such familial piety within the public expression of faith. However, he goes on to point out that the insights and language of familial piety did eventually influence Israel's public expression of faith, e.g., in the individual laments of the Psalter. See *Persönliche Frömmigkeit und offizielle Religion: Religionsinterner Pluralismus in Israel und Babylon* (Calwer Theologische Monographien A/9; Stuttgart: Calwer Verlag, 1979).

[18] R. E. Murphy has made significant contributions to the manner of appropriating Israel's Psalms by the modern believer. See "Psalms," *JBC* 35:18, pp. 575-576; "Israel's Psalms: Contributions to Today's Prayer Style," *Review for Religious* 34 (1975) 113-120; *The Psalms, Job*, 47-57; "The Faith of the Psalmist," *Int* 34 (1980) 229-239.

Praise him with timbrel and dance; praise him with strings and pipe! Praise him with sounding cymbals (Ps 150:4-5).

C. Westermann has remarked that in western theology we talk *about* God whereas in the Psalms, especially in the laments, we talk *to* God.[19] Both the symbolic language and the I-thou relationship[20] challenge us to adopt new prayer habits. We are asked to be open to this world of images and symbols that we may participate in the prayer of Israel's poets and thus add our voice to this ongoing chorus of praise and petition.

In praying the Psalms we thus share the experience of the poet which is an authentic encounter with God. In communicating that experience, the poet eschews logic, preferring to capture its intensity by means of images and symbols. It is these images and symbols that speak to our prayer needs. We are urged to be tantalized by the poet's perception so that we may immerse ourselves in his creative words. At the same time these words will become a springboard for enriching our own particular circumstances. The poet's description of awe, fear, trust, love, hate, etc. becomes ours in a special way when we allow it to touch our world. The universal language of images and symbols is thereby concretized in our unique setting. To reactivate our dormant poetic faculties is to enhance our prayer.[21]

---

[19] C. Westermann, "The Role of the Lament in the Theology of the Old Testament," *Int* 28 (1974) 22. This also appears in Westermann's *Praise and Lament in the Psalms* (Atlanta: John Knox, 1980) 261. For the significance of the stylized, direct speech of the Psalms see W. Brueggemann, *The Creative Word: Canon as a Model for Biblical Education* (Philadelphia: Fortress, 1982) 92-102.

[20] See M. Buber, *I and Thou* (2d ed.; New York: Scribner, 1958).

[21] See L. Alonso Schökel, *The Inspired Word*, 28-30, 159-162, 167-168, 202, 229-230. *Treinta Salmos*, 18-33. The following also insist on the poetic character of the Psalms as the key to appreciating them: T. Merton, *Bread in the Wilderness* (New York: New Directions, 1953) 45-47; *Praying the Psalms* (Collegeville, Minnesota: The Liturgical Press, 1956) 16; C. S. Lewis, *Reflections on the Psalms* (New York: Harcourt, Brace, & World, 1958) 3.

The rhythm of human life

In a brilliant essay W. Brueggemann presses the question of the function of the Psalms.[22] Granting the different types of psalms with their corresponding life setting,[23] he asks about the use that Israel made of these prayers. Since those responsible for the Psalter were intelligent people and proceeded in a reasonable manner, what were they attempting to achieve? Once an answer is forthcoming, then we may ask: "what are we to do?"[24]

Brueggemann next observes that human experience is variable. We know those moments when equilibrium and balance are the rule. There are no sudden devastating shocks or upsetting blows. We enjoy the security that our past has provided. Since balance and harmony prevail, we tend to believe that "God's in his heaven, all's right with the world." However, we also experience those times when our secure and seemingly impregnable world utterly collapses. The tried and true dicta of the past simply will not work. We attempt to rebuild our world but we do it the old-fashioned way. The results are deeper despair and greater disillusionment. Depending on our willingness to let go, we may then

---

On the topic of symbolism see O. Keel, *The Symbolism of the Biblical World: Ancient Near Eastern Iconography and the Book of Psalms* (New York: Seabury, 1978); L. Monloubou, *L'imaginaire des psalmistes* (Lectio Divina; Paris: Cerf, 1980).

[22] W. Brueggemann, "Psalms and the Life of Faith: A Suggested Typology of Function," *JSOT* 17 (1980) 3-32.

[23] For a summary of the form-critical approach to the Psalms by its pioneer see H. Gunkel, *The Psalms: A Form-Critical Introduction* (Facet Books — Biblical Series; Philadelphia: Fortress, 1972). For an assessment of this approach and recent literature on the topic see E. Gerstenberger, "Psalms," *Old Testament Form Criticism* (ed. J. Hayes; Trinity University Monograph Series in Religion 2; San Antonio: Trinity University, 1974) 179-223.

[24] A significant influence on Brueggemann has been the work of P. Ricoeur dealing with the role of language in the life of faith. The following publications by Ricoeur are noteworthy: *Freud and Philosophy* (New Haven: Yale University, 1970); *Conflict of Interpretations* (Evanston: Northwestern University, 1974); "Biblical Hermeneutics," *Semeia* 4 (1975) 29-148; *Interpretation Theory* (Fort Worth: Texas Christian University, 1976).

begin to reach a point where we are willing to admit newness into our lives. It is not a newness built on our own effort and predicated on our own premises. It is a newness that comes as gift or grace. If we are willing to run the risk of a world now built on other premises, we overcome our discouragement and frustration by reaching out to the promise of Another. Though we may regain what we had "before the fall," we are different people. We have experienced the fall and consequently our values and preconceptions have shifted. Brueggemann labels these three stages: (a) orientation; (b) disorientation; (c) reorientation.

The final form of Job may serve as a paradigm of this process. In the prose prologue (Job 1-2) Job is the model of virtue. He lives in a very secure world where all needs are met and where even tragedies can be absorbed. However, for most mortals this is never-never land. In the words of R. A. F. MacKenzie Job is someone we can admire but not identify with.[25] This is Job in orientation. However, at the start of chapter 3 Job begins to get caught up in the imbalance of life. Its rhyme or reason (orientation) has passed. This is the time for the invective and taunts of the poetic dialogues (Job 3:27, 29-31). Job's world has collapsed and he is tempted to reconstruct it with the theology of orientation. This is Job in disorientation. Finally in the prose epilogue (Job 42:7-17) Job is changed. He has reached out to embrace a newness not based on his earlier categories. This is now a Job we can not only admire but also identify with. Job has become one of us because of disorientation. This is Job in reorientation.

Brueggemann has suggested that certain types of psalms fit these different stages.[26] Thus there are psalms that speak to our needs, that reflect "where we're at." This book is an effort to range various psalm types according to our (or our community's) place in the process of orientation-

---

[25] R. A. F. MacKenzie, "The Transformation of Job," *BTB* 9 (1979) 52.
[26] W. Brueggemann, "Psalms and the Life of Faith," 6-10.

disorientation-reorientation. Under orientation there are hymns or psalms of descriptive praise (chapter 2), psalms of confidence or trust (chapter 3), wisdom psalms (chapter 4), and royal psalms (chapter 5). Under disorientation there are laments, both individual and communal (chapter 6) Finally under reorientation there are thanksgivings or psalms of declarative praise, both individual and communal (chapter 7).

A few cautions are in order. First, given the size of the Psalter and the limitations of this book, only some psalms representative of the type under consideration can be given. However, other psalms which fit the category are noted. Second, this orientation-disorientation-reorientation process suggested by Brueggemann is not a Procrustean bed that can reduce all of the Psalter to the desired stage. Rather, it helps to control many of the Psalms and hopefully facilitates our approach to prayer. Third, humans experience cycles in their prayer life, just as they experience cycles in other dimensions of life.[27] If reorientation begins to become the normal state of an individual, the reorientation is then orientation. Fourth, we are urged to pray all the psalms. If we exercise a canon within a canon, for example, by focusing only on psalms of orientation, we may cease to be aware of others who are reeling from the trauma of disorientation. Hence we may realistically and legitimately pray the psalms of disorientation despite our own state of security. Covenant demands such reaching out. Or — to adopt the stance of Paul — "If one member suffers, all suffer together" (1 Cor 12:26).[28]

---

[27]See J. Goldingay, "The Dynamic Cycle of Praise and Prayer in the Psalms," *JSOT* 20 (1981) 85-90. Note also Brueggemann's reply: "Response to John Goldingay's 'The Dynamic Cycle of Praise and Prayer,'" *JSOT* 22 (1982) 141-142.

[28]See T. Worden, *The Psalms Are Christian Prayer*, 38-40.520

2

In Praise of Dependence
The Psalms of Descriptive Praise

Ancients versus moderns

In the ancient Near East the gods were in charge. They provided the order and security without which human life was judged to be impossible. The deliberations of the divine assembly regulated all aspects of the lives of men, women, and children. In turn, humans were called upon to acknowledge this total dependence by singing hymns to their gods.[1] Such hymns articulated in praise form the supreme virtue of dependence.

In our age dependence is no longer the supreme virtue. It is clearly autonomy or independence. Hence praise does not come easily to our lips. Our human proclivity is to be locked into ourselves, into our private little world where no one may intrude except to acknowledge our autonomy. We suffer, therefore, from the debilitating disease of egomania.

Even if we manage to admit the centrality of God in our lives, we find it exceedingly difficult to grant center stage to

[1]See B. W. Anderson, *Out of the Depths*, 24-31; H. H. Guthrie, *Israel's Sacred Songs*, 61-71. For an ongoing refinement of this conception in biblical prayer see M. Greenberg, "On the Refinement of the Conception of Prayer in Hebrew Scriptures," *Association for Jewish Studies Review* 1 (1976) 57-92.

other humans. We will confess only one Creator, thereby eliminating all co-creators. We may unshackle ourselves to praise the Creator but we will not, indeed at times cannot advance to the point of praising the Creator's presence in others. Though we are surrounded by ample evidence of the goodness of others and hence the reflection of the Creator, we choose to set limits to our God's capacity to reveal himself in others.[2]

Hymns or psalms of descriptive praise = hymn

C. Westermann distinguishes two forms of psalms of praise: (a) psalms of descriptive praise which are properly called hymns; and (b) psalms of declarative praise which many label thanksgivings. Though both praise God, their focus is different. Psalms of descriptive praise envision an ongoing situation and, therefore, ongoing security. On the other hand, psalms of declarative praise assert what has recently occurred, i.e., God's new provision or interruption that takes the form of miracle or wonder.[3] A common

---

[2] Concerning a reaction to this theology in the Book of Qoheleth see W. Zimmerli, "The Place and Limit of the Wisdom in the Framework of the Old Testament," *Scottish Journal of Theology* 17 (1964) 146-158, esp. 155-158. This has been reprinted in: *Studies in Ancient Israelite Wisdom* (ed. J. L. Crenshaw; New York: Ktav, 1976) 314-326, esp. 323-326. See also J. F. Craghan, *Love and Thunder* 175-183. With regard to this theology in the Book of Jonah see T. E. Fretheim, *The Message of Jonah: A Theological Commentary* (Minneapolis: Augsburg, 1977) 22-28; "Jonah and Theodicy," *ZAW* 90 (1978) 227-237; J. F. Craghan, *Love and Thunder*, 185-194; B. Vawter, *Job and Jonah: Questioning the Hidden God* (New York: Paulist, 1983) 114-116.

[3] C. Westermann, *Praise and Lament*, 17-18, 30-33, 34-35; "Psalms, Book of," *IDBSup*, 707. Westermann's division has not met with general acceptance. Brueggemann ("Psalms and the Life of Faith," 9) makes the following distinction: "Thus Westermann's proposal may be open to question in terms of *form* but *functionally* on target" (author's italics)." F. Crüsemann (*Studien zur Formgeschichte von Hymnus und Danklied in Israel* [Wissenchaftliche Monographien zum Alten und Neuen Testament 32; Neukirchen-Vluyn: Neukirchener Verlag, 1969] distinguishes two totally independent types of hymns. Moreover, as opposed to Westermann, Crüsemann maintains that there is a clear distinction between the psalm of descriptive praise (hymn) and the psalm of declarative praise (thanksgiving). Perhaps the most telling critique of Westermann's position has come from H. H.

feature of the psalm of descriptive praise is the Hebrew participle, implying that God is one who characteristically does such and such. Psalms of descriptive praise underline God's ongoing creative activity in one dimension or another.

The structure of the psalm of descriptive praise is relatively simple.[4] In the introduction the psalmist expresses his intention to praise God or he may invite others to join in the praise. In the main section the psalmist offers reasons or motives for such praise. They are typically introduced by the conjunction "for" (*kî* in Hebrew). However, as C. Stuhlmueller remarks, this conjunction is more like our English exclamation point. The purpose of the main section "is more to sustain wonder and adoration in God's presence, to involve the worshipping community in God's glorious action."[5] In the conclusion the psalmist usually restates elements found in the introduction.

Since psalms of descriptive praise dwell on God's ongoing care for his creation, they express harmony, stability, and balance. Against the background of the ancient Near East such psalms acclaim "what turned out to be the nature of the god on the basis of the annual and monthly and daily

Guthrie (*Theology as Thanksgiving: From Israel's Psalms to the Church's Eucharist* [New York: Seabury, 1981] 1-30) who points out, *inter alia*, that the form of the Hebrew verb in hymns is participial whereas in thanksgivings the form is finite. He further demonstrates that the difference in form is basically a difference in theology: "The ruler of the cosmos had turned out to be a deity who chose to be involved and active in the events constituting the life and history of a people, whose actions were directly a part of a people's remembered heritage, praise of whom demanded the recitation in finite verb forms of how Israel had been delivered from slavery and oppression in a remembered course of events. Thanksgiving, *todah*, was demanded as the appropriate praise of the ruler of the cosmos, for *Yahweh* had turned out to be that ruler" (author's italics - 22).

[4]See C. Westermann, *Praise and Lament*, 122-130.

[5]C. Stuhlmueller, *Psalms* 1.35. For Crüsemann this particle has the function of introducing direct discourse. Hence it is not the reason for the praise but the carrying out of the praise demanded by such imperatives as Exodus 15:21. See F. Crüsemann, *Studien zur Formgeschichte*, 33; also E. Gerstenberger, "Psalms," 209-210.

realities in the cycles of nature."[6] As a result, they clearly exemplify the mind-set of orientation with its orderly flow of events. In terms of prayer these psalms challenge us to withstand the centripetal force of our ego and thus sing the goodness of Another who continues to create — so often in and through others. The more human we become, i.e., the more prayerful we become, the more we are open to God and God's goodness in others. Stated negatively, a life devoid of praise is not a human life.[7]

Psalm 8[8]

O Lord, our Lord
how majestic is thy name in all the earth!
Thou whose glory above the heavens is chanted
[2]by the mouth of babes and infants,
    thou hast founded a bulwark because of thy foes,
        to still the enemy and the avenger.
[3]When I look at thy heavens, the work of thy fingers,
        the moon and the stars which thou hast established;
[4]what is man that thou art mindful of him,
        and the son of man that thou dost care for him?

[5]Yet thou hast made him little less than God,
        and dost crown him with glory and honor.
[6]Thou hast given him dominion over
        the works of thy hands;
    thou hast put all things under his feet

---

[6] H. H. Guthrie, *Theology as Thanksgiving*, 6.

[7] For the implications of praise in a truly human approach to the Psalter and life see C. S. Lewis, *Reflections on the Psalms*, 93-98.

[8] See A. Weiser, *The Psalms*, 139-146; H.-J. Kraus, *Psalmen* (4th ed.; BKAT 15/1-2 Neukirchen-Vluyn: Neukirchener Verlag, 1972) 65-73; R. Tournay, "Le Psaume VIII et la doctrine biblique du nom," *Revue biblique* 78 (1971) 18-30; K. Gouders, "Gottes Schöpfung und Auftrag des Menschen," *Bibel und Leben* 14 (1973) 164-179; W. Rudolph, "'Aus dem Munde der jungen Kinder und Säuglinge . . .' Psalm 8:3," *Beiträge zur Alttestamentlichen Theologie: Festschrift für Walther Zimmerli* (ed. H. Donner et al.; Göttingen: Vandenhoeck & Ruprecht, 1977) 388-396.

7all sheep and oxen,
and also the beasts of the field,
8the birds of the air, and the fish of the sea,
dhatever passes along the paths of the sea,
9O LORD, our Lord,
how majestic is thy name in all the earth!

This psalm is a perfect inclusion, i.e., it repeats at the end (v 9) the expression used in the beginning (v 1a): "O Lord, our Lord, how majestic is thy name in all the earth!" The expression creates the climate of contemplation, beckoning to the audience to acknowledge the majesty of the God of Israel in the body of the psalm (vv 1b-8). However, the psalmist soon interjects a disconcerting question. If contemplation of the heavens with the moon and stars (v 3) provokes a cry of admiration, then the vision of humans (frail humanity is the poet's concern) in verse 4 seems to provoke a cry of desperation. Such humans occupy a position slightly below that of God (RSV) or, more likely, below that of the divine members of the heavenly court (see Ps 82:1). What is involved is the risk of creation.

In verse 2 the author sets up a contrast: (a) babes and infants; and (b) foes, the enemy, and the avenger. The author next heightens the contrast by dwelling on the royalty of humans. He describes them by mentioning the typical qualities of a king in verse 5: crown, glory, and honor.9

9See B. W. Anderson, "Human Dominion Over Nature," *Biblical Studies in Contemporary Thought* (ed. M. Ward; Burlington, Vermont: Trinity College Biblical Institute, 1975) 27-45, esp. 32-37. For the implications of royalty and humanness in Genesis 2-3 see H. A. Kenik, "Towards a Biblical Basis for Creation Theology," *Western Spirituality: Historical Roots, Ecumenical Routes* (ed. M. Fox; Notre Dame, Indiana: Fides/Claretian, 1979) 27-75, esp. 48-61. For the significance of the interrelation of royal power, creation, and wisdom, especially in view of human maturity and freedom, note the following studies by W. Brueggemann: "David and His Theologian," *CBQ* 30 (1968) 156-181; "The Trusted Creature," *CBQ* 31 (1969) 484-498; "The Triumphalist Tendency in Exegetical History," *JAAR* 30 (1970) 367-380; "Kingship and Chaos," *CBQ* 33 (1971) 317-332; *In Man We Trust* (Richmond: John Knox, 1972); "Life and Death in Tenth Century Israel," *JAAR* 40 (1972) 96-109; "On Trust and Freedom, A Study of Faith in the Succession Narrative," *Int* 26 (1972) 3-19.

In verses 6-8 he develops this regal character by picturing humans after the manner of Genesis 1. Humans, therefore, share in God's own glory so that they may be his representatives on earth. The God of this psalm is one who can delegate, not hoard power and thereby escape the danger of relegating humans to the level of puppets. However, the contrast of verse 2 still lingers. Which way will humans go with their regal power? Will they be babes and infants, or will they be foes, the enemy, and the avenger?

This psalm raises in poetic form the dilemma of the Garden of Eden. Obviously the writer knows that humans have a tendency to renounce their creatureliness and assume the arrogant airs of absolute monarchy. We all like to play God, thereby making ourselves the center of the universe and the absolute norm by which good and evil are determined.[10] However as L. Alonso Schökel notes,[11] the opposite of rebellion is the ministry of praise. The attitude opposed to vengeful rebellion is the attitude of the child. Here we have a world of happiness, discovery, and affirmation. Instead of being rebellious giants, we humans are exhorted to be infants discovering and subsequently praising our God.[12]

To praise God is to acknowledge God's risk in creating. However, to continue to praise is to opt for the status of responsible kings and queens with its typical order of orientation. To praise this God is to realize that we have obliga-

---

[10] See W. M. Clark, "A Legal Background for the Yahwist's Use of 'Good and Evil' in Genesis 2-3," *JBL* 88 (1969) 266-278; G. W. Coats, "The God of Death," *Int* 29 (1975) 227-239; L. Alonso Schökel, "Sapiential and Covenant Themes in Genesis 2-3," *Studies in Ancient Israelite Wisdom*, 468-480.

[11] L. Alonso Schökel, *Treinta Salmos*, 71.

[12] A. George (*Praying the Psalms*, 62) comments on this attitude in the New Testament: "Jesus can use this Old Testament prayer just as it is with its wondrous praise, its gratitude to the Father who reveals himself to the childlike (Matt 11:25). There is something of this idea in the argument which he draws from this psalm in answering the High Priests of the Temple: children recognize God's messenger more quickly than the wise men (Matt 21:16)." For a similar observation in the context of adult education see G. Moran, *Interplay: A Theory of Religion and Education* (Winona, Minnesota: Saint Mary's, 1981) 117.

tions to this God and this God's creation. "Only when one understands man in the light of the man, Jesus Christ, can he see what God intended humanity to be — not a man who was freed from the threats of daily life, but one who himself entered for a while into the full sufferings of humanity in order to bring life to all men."[13] Psalm 8 challenges us to be the authors of life, not the proliferators of death.

Psalm 29[14]

> [1] Ascribe to the Lord,O heavenly beings,
>   ascribe to the LORD glory and strength.
> [2] Ascribe to the LORD the glory of his name;
>   worship the LORD in holy array.
> [3] The voice of the LORD is upon the waters;
>   the God of glory thunders,
>   the LORD, upon many waters.
> [4] The voice of the LORD is powerful,
>   the voice of the LORD is full of majesty.
>
> [5] The voice of the LORD breaks the cedars,
>   the LORD breaks the cedars of Lebanon.
> [6] He makes Lebanon to skip like a calf,
>   and Sirion like a young wild ox.
>
> [7] The voice of the LORD flashes forth flames of fire.
> [8] The voice of the LORD shakes the wilderness,
>   the LORD shakes the wilderness of Kadesh.
> [9] The voice of the LORD makes the oaks to whirl,
>   and strips the forests bare;
>   and in his temple all cry, "Glory!"
>
> [10] The LORD sits enthroned over the flood;
>   the LORD sits enthroned as king for ever.
> [11] May the LORD give strength to his people!
>   May the LORD bless his people with peace!

---

[13] B. S. Childs, "Psalm 8 in the Context of the Christian Canon," *Int* 23 (1969) 30.

[14] See A. Weiser, *The Psalms*, 259-265; H. –J. Kraus, *Psalmen*, 233-239; H. H. Guthrie, *Israel's Sacred Songs*, 75-80; *Theology as Thanksgiving*, 3-4, 14, 26-29.

There is a consensus among scholars that this psalm was originally a pagan composition extolling the Canaanite god, Baal, the weather god who through storms and rains brings fertility to the earth.[15] Here the imagery deals with the end of the summer drought and the renewal of life and fertility with the arrival of the fall rains. The heavenly beings mentioned in verse 1 were originally the minor gods of the Canaanite pantheon. In appropriating this hymn for her worship, Israel substituted the name of her god, Yahweh, for that of Baal. Hence Yahweh is acknowledged as the cosmic lord who meets the fertility needs of his people.[16] Consequently the psalm is a perfect example of the movement of orientation, viz., Yahweh's recurring goodness in the form of rain.

In appropriating this pagan composition, Israel impressed upon it her own view of the transcendent Yahweh — yet a Yahweh who entered into her history. For example, the wilderness in verse 8 was originally "the holy wilderness" but now it is historicized as "Kadesh," i.e., the sanctuary associated with the making of the covenant. Nonetheless the transcendence of Yahweh remains paramount.

Alonso Schökel has shown that after the introduction (vv 1-2) the poet tries to recreate in the main section (vv 3-9) a mighty tempest as a theophany, i.e., a manifestation of God, especially of God's power.[17] He recreates this scene by means of words. In the storm which is real the poet senses a higher power which has revealed itself. This revelation provokes both fear and fascination. The storm begins either in the Mediterranean Sea or the heavenly ocean (v 3), viz., the ocean above the firmament-protected earth. In verses 5-9a this powerful storm now invades the earth. It leaps over Lebanon, goes under Sirion (the Phoenician name for Mount Hermon), passes to the wilderness, and penetrates

---

[15] See F. M. Cross, *Canaanite Myth and Hebrew Epic: Essays in the History of the Religion of Israel* (Cambridge: Harvard University, 1973) 151-157, 160-162.

[16] For a description of the psalmist's manner of appropriating this Canaanite composition see L. Alonso Schökel, *The Inspired Word*, 199-200.

[17] L. Alonso Schökel, *Treinta Salmos*, 126-127.

the forest. The breaking of cedars, the flames of fire, the convulsing earth, and the tireless voice coalesce to provide an image of power.

This divine power, however, demands recognition.[18] In verse 9b all acknowledge Yahweh's "glory," viz., that quality by which God manifests his presence on earth.[19] Here it is a regal quality. In verse 10 Yahweh sits enthroned in his temple which is above the firmament ("the flood"). In the Jerusalem temple, therefore, Israel experiences in an exceedingly tangible way the transcendent One whose dwelling is elsewhere.[20] At the same time this presence is linked to something concrete. Peace (v 11) is not merely the cessation of hostilities but the condition of wholeness whereby living becomes celebration.

The power of this psalm must impact our technological world. It must put us in contact with the power of our transcendent God. Despite our computer expertise we have not outgrown our ability to experience the mystery of God.[21] Here is an awesome God who is not subject to the caprices of our programmers. Here is a God who speaks to us through nature and other humans. Prayer must become that enterprise whereby we discover the manifold presence

[18] A. Heschel (*Man's Quest for God*, 92) remarks: "It is man who is the cantor of the universe, and in whose life the secret of cosmic prayer is disclosed."

[19] See F. M. Cross, *Canaanite Myth and Hebrew Epic*, 165-167; G. E. Mendenhall, "The Mask of Yahweh," *The Tenth Generation: The Origins of the Biblical Tradition* (Baltimore: The Johns Hopkins University, 1973) 32-66.

[20] S. Terrien has constructed a monumental biblical theology around the theme of presence. In *The Elusive Presence: Towards a New Biblical Theology* (Religious Perspectives 26; New York: Harper & Row, 1978) xxvii he writes: "The Deity of the Hebrew-Christian Scriptures escapes man's grasp and manipulation, but man is aware of the presence of that Deity in such a powerful way that he finds through it a purpose in the universe; he confers upon his own existence a historical meaning; and he attunes his selfhood to an ultimate destiny." See also R. E. Clements, *God and Temple: The Idea of the Divine Presence in Ancient Israel* (Oxford: Blackwell, 1965); R. de Vaux, "The Presence and Absence of God in History According to the Old Testament," *The Presence of God* (ed. P. Benoit et al.; Concilium 50; New York: Paulist, 1969) 7-20; W. Brueggemann, "Presence of God, Cultic," *IDBSup*, 680-683.

[21] See R. Otto, *The Idea of the Holy* (2d ed.; London: Oxford University, 1950) 25-40.

of this God once again. With such rediscoveries we enter upon a world where all needs are met and hence living is truly celebration. Such is the task of prayer. "To pray is to take notice of the wonder, to regain a sense of the mystery that animates all beings, the divine margin in all attainments."[22]

Psalm 19[23]

The heavens are telling the glory of God;
   and the firmament proclaims his handiwork.
[2]Day to day pours forth speech,
   and night to night declares knowledge.
[3]There is no speech, nor are there words;
   their voice is not heard;
[4]yet their voice goes out through all the earth,
   and their words to the end of the world.
In them he has set a tent for the sun,
[5]which comes forth like a bridegroom leaving his
   chamber,
   and like a strong man runs its course with joy.
[6]Its rising is from the end of the heavens,
   and its circuit to the end of them;
   and there is nothing hid from its heat.

[7]The law of the LORD is perfect,
   reviving the soul;
the testimony of the LORD is sure,
   making wise the simple;
[8]the precepts of the LORD are right,
   rejoicing the heart;
the commandment of the LORD is pure,
   enlightening the eyes;
[9]the fear of the LORD is clean,
   enduring for ever;

---

[22] A. Heschel, *Man's Quest for God*, 5.

[23]See A. Weiser, *The Psalms*, 197-204; H.-J. Kraus, *Psalmen*, 152-161; H. H. Guthrie, *Israel's Sacred Songs*, 188-190.

> the ordinances of the LORD are true,
>   and righteous altogether.
> [10]More to be desired are they than gold,
>   even much fine gold;
> sweeter also than honey
>   and drippings of the honeycomb.
>
> [11]Moreover by them is thy servant warned;
>   in keeping them there is great reward.
> [12]But who can discern his errors?
>   Clear thou me from hidden faults.
> [13]Keep back thy servant also from presumptuous sins;
>   let them not have dominion over me!
> Then I shall be blameless,
>   and innocent of great transgression.
>
> [14]Let the words of my mouth and the
>   meditation of my heart
> be acceptable in thy sight,
>   O LORD, my rock and my redeemer.

This prayer consists of two distinct but complementary psalms. The first and older psalm is verses 1-6 which is a psalm of descriptive praise. The second and younger psalm is verses 7-14 which is basically a wisdom psalm. The beauty of this composition is that the second psalm develops the theme of divine presence by reflecting on God's directives and Israel's traditions.

The first psalm was originally a pagan paean honoring the Semitic god El (translated "God" in verse 1). The heavenly phenomena, especially the sun, proclaim inaudibly yet realistically the praise of El. In its Israelite form Yahweh, of course, becomes the object of praise. In Alonso Schökel's view[24] the heavens and the firmament (v 1) are personified spaces while day and night (v 2) are personified times. The activity of all four consists in speaking. The earth functions

---

[24] Alonso Schökel, *Treinta Salmos*, 96-97.

as the great audience hall that listens to the heavenly discourse. Though words are not employed (v 3), the message reaches to the very ends of the world (v 4), communicating God's glory and actions (v 1).

The sun god in the pagan myth had a tent where he spent the night with his beloved and from which he departed in the morning to resume his circuit with renewed vigor and vitality. In the Israelite adaptation the sun does not speak. Instead, it carries along and repeats the message of the heavens and the firmament.[25]

The second psalm, far from destroying the beauty of the first, now takes the theme of God's presence in another direction. It is not only nature that announces in ineffable speech the divine presence. It is also God's torah (translated "law" in RSV), i.e., God's wise instruction including all of God's directives and Israel's traditions.[26] However, this torah is intelligible language that articulates God's will. Like the sun, God's revelation enlightens and brightens God's people (v 8), even to the point of illuminating one's inadvertent faults ("errors" in verse 12).

In its final form this psalm is not an "either-or" but a "both-and." It is not a question of finding God's presence only in nature to the exclusion of revelation or vice versa. It is, rather, a matter of finding God both in the beauty of nature and in the beauty of the revealed word. As Stuhlmueller aptly puts it, "the liturgy of the universe and that of the sanctuary should echo one another, so that one helps to appreciate the other."[27]

At Prayer we are invited to listen to the inaudible but real God who commands the works of creation to communicate the depth of his love. At prayer we are also urged to listen to

---

[25] Ibid., 98.

[26] See J. Jensen, *The Use of tôrâ by Isaiah: His Debate with the Wisdom Tradition* (Catholic Biblical Quarterly Monograph Series 3; Washington, D. C.: The Catholic Biblical Association of America, 1973) 3-27.

[27] C. Stuhlmueller, *Psalms*, 1. 137.

the ongoing revelation of God's concern. In turn, we are challenged to orchestrate with nature and proclaim: "He is good, very good." We are invited as well to let the revealed word have an impact on our total person (translated "soul" in verse 7)[28] Ultimately both forms of manifestation contribute to the orderliness of our world. Ours is thereby a world made firm by nature and solidified by the spoken word.

Psalm 113[29]

> Praise the LORD!
> Praise, O servants of the LORD,
> > praise the name of the LORD!
>
> [2]Blessed be the name of the LORD
> > from this time forth and for evermore!
> [3]From the rising of the sun to its setting
> > the name of the LORD is to be praised!
> [4]The LORD is high above all nations,
> > and his glory above the heavens!
>
> [5]Who is like the LORD our God,
> > who is seated on high,
> [6]who looks far down
> > upon the heavens and the earth?
>
> [7]He raises the poor from the dust,
> > and lifts the needy from the ash heap,
> [8]to make them sit with princes,
> > with the princes of his people.
> [9]He gives the barren woman a home,
> > making her the joyous mother of children.
> Praise the LORD!

---

[28] For the significance of a sound biblical anthropology see J. Blenkinsopp, "On Saving One's Soul," *A Sketchbook of Biblical Theology* (New York: Herder & Herder, 1968) 94-104.

[29] See A. Weiser, *The Psalms*, 704-708; H. -J. Kraus, *Psalmen*, 775-777.

Creation is not the only motive for praising the God of
Israel. Yahweh's actions on behalf of his people are equally
significant.[30] This implies that Yahweh's heavenly court is
not a type of Berlin Wall, eliminating concern as to how the
other half lives. Indeed the covenant demands that this God
be inextricably bound up with this people and be committed
to action on their behalf.

The psalm opens by inviting Yahweh's servants to praise
their God. Although "servants" (v 1) can refer to cultic
employees, it also extends to all Israel (see Ps 69:35-36). In
the first three verses the name of Yahweh is accentuated.
This name is coextensive with the person of Israel's God.
According to Exodus 3:13-17 and 6:2-8 the revelation of the
divine name takes place in the setting of Egyptian bondage.
To mention Yahweh is to conjure up the picture of a God
who liberates slaves and offers them a future in a promised
land. The expression "from the rising of the sun to its
setting" (v 3) refers to the Diaspora, viz., those scattered
throughout the ancient Near East after the exile. However,
where the divine name is revered, there the divine person is
involved.

We never stand so tall as when we stoop to help a little
child. This psalmist develops this theology in the body of the
poem (vv 4-9a) by underlining the chasm separating Yahweh and his servants. However, it is a chasm that can be
overcome. To be sure, Yahweh is high above all nations (v
4). He is also incomparable as he occupies his lofty throne (v
5). Nevertheless he bends down to inspect the situation in
the heavens and on the earth (v 6). But the inspection is not
another committee report, it is directed to action.

Who are the beautiful people? According to this psalm
there are at least two categories: (a) the poor and the needy;
and (b) barren women. In both cases reversal is the order of

---

[30] For the value and manner of use of Israel's historical traditions in the Psalms
see J. Kühlewein, *Geschichte in den Psalmen* (Calwer Theologische Monographien A/2; Stuttgart: Calwer Verlag, 1973).

the day. The One on high (v 4) raises on high the poor and the needy (v 7). Moreover, the Enthroned One (v 5) now enthrones these poor and needy. They occupy seats along with the politicos of God's people. The movement from dust and ash heap to throne is possible because the God of the covenant is a committed God.[31] With regard to the barren women one must note that in the sociology of Israel a woman found fulfillment by becoming a wife and mother. She contributed to the covenant community by bearing children. The accounts of Israel's matriarchs are sufficient to point up the plight of the unfulfilled woman (see Genesis 16; 30). But thanks to Yahweh's intervention the barren are no longer sullen. They break out into paroxysms of joy because Yahweh has removed the stigma by giving them children (v 9; see 1 Sam 2:5). It is only fitting that the psalm should conclude as it began: "Praise the Lord."

This psalm does not offer a taxative list of the down and out. However, it does suggest to our imagination that wherever the down and out are helped, the name of Yahweh is present and deserves recognition. In praying such psalms, we are to acknowledge those individuals who reach out from their security to lend a helping hand. Divine presence takes many forms. To help fellow humans in any way is to make God's name contagious and hence worthy of praise. At prayer we are urged to break free from the grip of our ego to focus on those who demonstrate freedom by giving themselves. To praise them is to demolish the barriers we erect even in prayer. To pray to this God is to be involved with this God's people —everyone.

---

[31] For the connotations of royalty in the dust motif of Genesis 2:7a see W. Brueggemann, "From Dust to Kingship," *ZAW* 84 (1972) 1-18. For a possible royal allusion in the breath of the nostril motif in Genesis 2:7b see W. Wifall, "The Breath of His Nostrils: Gen 2, 7b," *CBQ* 36 (1974) 237-240.

Psalm 65[32]

Praise is due to thee,
O God, in Zion;
and to thee shall vows be performed,
[2]O thou who hearest prayer!
To thee shall all flesh come
[3]on account of sins.
When our transgressions prevail over us,
thou dost forgive them.
[4]Blessed is he whom thou dost
choose and bring near,
to dwell in thy courts!
We shall be satisfied with the goodness
of thy house, thy holy temple!

[5]By dread deeds thou dost answer us
with deliverance,
O God of our salvation,
who art the hope of all the ends of the earth,
and of the farthest seas;
[6]who by thy strength hast established the mountains,
being girded with might;
[7]who dost still the roaring of the seas,
the roaring of their waves,
the tumult of the peoples;
[8]so that those who dwell at earth's farthest bounds
are afraid at thy signs;
thou makest the outgoings of the morning and the evening
to shout for joy.

[9]Thou visitest the earth and waterest it,
thou greatly enrichest it;
the river of God is full of water;
thou providest their grain,
for so thou hast prepared it.
[10]Thou waterest its furrows abundantly,

---

[32]See A. Weiser, *The Psalms*, 460-466; H. –J. Kraus, *Psalmen*, 448-454.

settling its ridges,
softening it with showers,
and blessing its growth.
[11]Thou crownest the year with thy bounty;
the tracks of thy chariot drip with fatness.
[12]The pastures of the wilderness drip,
the hills gird themselves with joy,
[13]the meadows clothe themselves with flocks,
the valleys deck themselves with grain,
they shout and sing together for joy.

Is Yahweh who has his temple in Zion (ancient Jerusalem, the eastern hill) and who controls the world and its history still interested in the day to day affairs of humans? The question may be put in another way. Besides the glory of the temple and the control of the universe is there another motive, indeed a more mundane motive, for breaking out into praise? The arrangement of this psalm offers an answer to these questions: (a) the attraction of Zion (vv 1-4); (b) Lord of the universe and history (vv 5-8); (c) Yahweh the farmer (vv 9-13).[33]

Mount Zion attracts praise and supplication. It beckons to all humans who wish to experience intimacy with God, especially because of human sinfulness (vv 1-3). In the heart of Zion, i.e., the temple, Israel recalls the mystery of her election — she has been chosen to enter God's house (v 4).

From Zion the psalmist now glances at the immense horizons of nature and history. The God of the sanctuary is the God of a people — indeed of an oppressed people (v 5). In verses 6-7 the psalmist recalls Yahweh's ongoing creative activity (participles are used here). Setting up the mountains and stilling the seas' roaring recall the story of creation whereby Yahweh overcame chaos and established cosmos. Even though the nations continue to be hostile by amassing their armies against Israel, Yahweh continues to keep them in check (v 8).

---

[33]See L. Alonso Schökel, *Treinta Salmos*, 257-261.

As Alonso Schökel notes,[34] the psalmist now gives the impression that God has left public and cosmic life to devote himself to farming (vv 9-10). The God who checks kingdoms, restrains oceans, and receives praise in the temple is also the one who farms the land. Thus the God of cult, the God of nature and history is also the concerned head of the household who provides for the needs of the family members (vv 11-12). The flocks on the hills and the grain in the valleys (v 13) are eloquent witness to Yahweh's concern for day to day needs. Against the background of such rich agricultural productivity the only adequate response is praise.

At prayer we are often tempted to focus on the great moments in our lives. Psalm 65, however, teaches us to look to the little moments as well, to the times of normalcy and humdrum affairs. We somehow feel reluctant to consider our jobs whether they be in the office or factory, at home, or on the farm, or wherever. Frequently we do not regard our positions as faith opportunities, i.e., the occasions to acknowledge a God who gives us health and talent. In the other direction we do not consider sufficiently those who meet our daily needs and hence those who work hand in hand with our God to provide for us. The tragedy is that we take human love for granted. Being in the temple or in control of the world seems more important, in this analogy, than being down on the farm. At prayer we are to count our blessings: our jobs, our abilities, but most of all our loved and loving ones. Prayer is the chance to reassess the humdrum and rediscover divine presence through love. Prayer makes us aware of the equilibrium that only love provides.

New Testament

Westermann observes that all psalms of descriptive praise are "governed by the tension of the relation to each other of the two statements that God is enthroned in majesty, and *yet*

---

[34] Ibid., 261.

is the one who is moved with compassion."[35] He further suggests that the two parts of the prologue of John (1:1-13 and 1:14-18) exemplify this tension.[36] The following remarks are intended as aids in praying this New Testament psalm of descriptive praise.

John 1:1-18

[1]In the beginning was the Word, and the Word was with God, and the Word was God. [2]He was in the beginning with God; [3]all things were made through him, and without him was not anything made that was made. [4]In him was life, and the life was the light of men. [5]The light shines in the darkness, and the darkness has not overcome it.

[6]There was a man sent from God, whose name was John. [7]He came for testimony, to bear witness to the light, that all might believe through him. [8]He was not the light, but came to bear witness to the light.

[9]The true light that enlightens every man was coming into the world. [10]He was in the world, and the world was made through him, yet the world knew him not. [11]He came to his own home, and his own people received him not.

[12]But to all who received him, who believed in his name, he gave power to become children of God; [13]who were born, not of blood nor of the will of the flesh nor of the will of man, but of God.

[14]And the Word became flesh and dwelt among us, full of grace and truth; we have beheld his glory, glory as of the only Son from the Father. [15](John bore witness to him, and cried, "This was he of whom I said, 'He who comes after me ranks before me, for he was before me.'") [16]And from his fulness have we all received, grace upon grace. [17]For the law was given through Moses; grace and

---

[35] C. Westermann, *Praise and Lament*, 133 (author's italics).
[36] Ibid., #86.

truth came through Jesus Christit. [18]No one has ever seen God; the only Son, who is in the bosom of the Father, he has made him known.

The prologue of John is a hymn that is probably an independent composition. Moreover, an editor or editors have added to the hymn by inserting materials (a) to explain the hymn more fully (vv 12b-13,17-18) and (b) to differentiate the roles of Jesus and the Baptist (vv 6-9,15). The title "Word" especially has wisdom overtones. The Word is thus like Lady Wisdom who is with God from the beginning (see Prov 8:22-23), who reflects God's glory and everlasting light (see Wis 7:25-26), and who provokes decisions (see Prov 8:17). The hymn begins with pre-creation and the Word's relationship to God. By creation ("in the beginning" of Genesis 1:1), which is also revelation, the Word has a claim on everyone. The effect of God's creative Word is the gift of eternal life. Although humans have failed through sin, the light continues to shine in darkness. Verses 11-12a describe the ministry of the Word and reach a crescendo in verse 14 where the Word is bound up with human history and human destiny.[37] Westermann notes that this descriptive praise is combined with declarative praise, viz., emphasis on God's new provision ("we have beheld his glory . . . . And from his fulness have we all received, . . .").[38]

At prayer we are compelled to recognize God's movement as ever going outward. In pre-creation there is the movement between God and the Word. In creation there is the movement between the Word and the world of nature and humans. In the incarnation there is the ultimate movement between the Word and fragile humanity. At prayer we are caught up in this series of movements. We see ourselves as the beneficiaries of God's ongoing goodness, we see other

[37] See R. E. Brown, *The Gospel According to John* (AB 29; Garden City, New York: Doubleday, 1966), 1. 3-37, 519-524; C. H. Dodd, *The Interpretation of the Fourth Gospel* (Cambridge: University Press, 1963) 263-285.

[38] C. Westermann, *Praise and Lament*, 133-134, #87.

humans as the empowered ambassadors of the Word. At prayer we are overawed by such a generous God who makes his world impact ours. In the presence of the Word we are left speechless. Balance and harmony means that the movement continues, becoming enfleshed in our prayer and our life style.

Summary of the theology of the hymns or the psalms of descriptive praise[39]

(1) These psalms speak of divine intervention and human interaction. They are an appeal to praise our God for the ongoingness of creation.

(2) They assume that we humans can recognize our God both in nature and history. They also assume that we are able to put aside our focus on self to concentrate on the Faithful One.

(3) They seek to celebrate the goodness of life because of the Giver of life.

(4) They exhort us to announce the death of egocentricity and proclaim the good news of theocentricity and anthropocentricity.

(5) They appeal to our ability to recognize the ongoingness of creation in other people. The God of Israel seldom chooses to operate alone. To praise the co-creators is to praise the Creator.

---

[39] Other psalms of descriptive praise include the following: 33, 47, 93, 95-100, 104-105, 114, 117, 134-136, 145-150.

3

In God We Trust
The Psalms of Trust or Confidence

Human progress versus divine reliance

Our technological age has witnessed unimagined wonders. The advances in medicine and the progress in aerospace engineering have established new parameters for human confidence. Generally speaking, we have grown to rely on things: pills, microcomputers, and word processors, to name only a few. Our world is one of instant replay. We press buttons or turn knobs and instantaneously retrieve past events. Whether we wish to admit it or not, we are in danger of total reliance on things.[1] Humans do not function, so we surmise, as adroitly or as perfectly as the products of our technological age. Our temptation is to mint a new American penny and substitute: "In things only do we trust."

To be sure, these are temptations and dangers but they are not insuperable. It need not be a question of human progress *versus* divine (or human) reliance. It can also be a question of human progress *and* divine (or human) reliance. In both instances we seek stability, harmony, and a regular flow in the rhythm of our lives. However, if we are to remain

---

[1]See A. Heschel's discussion of this problem in *Man's Quest for God*, xi-xiv.

45

genuinely human, we must be willing to run the risk of grounding ourselves in Another who in turn runs the risk of co-opting fellow humans for the enterprise of trust. We must be courageous enough to accept scientific advances and label them as good but also bold enough to acknowledge that we are caught up in the mystery of our God. The great heroes and heroines seem to be those who can opt for "both-and" rather than "either-or" in this great venture of modern living.

At prayer we experience the mystery of our God. We begin to realize that the good things of human technology must be a help in approaching our God, not a hindrance. We further perceive that things can never be a substitute for persons, whether our God or other humans. Our God is not a neatly packaged item of our productive ingenuity. Our God is one who freely enters into our lives and hence the lives of others. This is a God who offers us a greater challenge than that of our technological breakthroughs. This is a God who dares us to trust him, to be rooted in him, and thereby find stability and harmony in our lives. This is also a God who freely chooses to depend on humans in creating the climate of trust. The God of the Judeo-Christian tradition is one who provokes confidence.

Psalms of trust or confidence

S. Terrien describes these psalms in the following manner. They reflect a state of spiritual equilibrium and of satisfaction without smugness. In such psalms there is the unwavering, unruffled steadiness of complete trust. One senses here the sufficient God who neither hides nor haunts.[2] In these psalms certain motifs emerge, e.g., security like that of the infant nestling on its mother's lap (see Ps 131:2), intimacy with God (see Ps 16:9-11), absolute and

---

[2] S. Terrien, *The Elusive Presence*, 332.

exclusive attachment to this God (see Ps 125:1-2). This is indeed a world of orientation.

These psalms developed from the psalms of lament. They are the motives of confidence in the laments that have now become full-fledged psalms of their own. It is the predominance of the expressions of trust or confidence that distinguishes them from the laments. With regard to structure there is no consistent arrangement. Rather, the psalmist reiterates the different images and symbols of the all-encompassing presence of the God of Israel.[3]

Psalm 23[4]

> The LORD is my shepherd, I shall not want;
> 2   he makes me lie down in green pastures.
> He leads me beside still waters;
> 3   he restores my soul.
> He leads me in paths of righteousness
>   for his name's sake.
>
> 4 Even though I walk through the valley
>   of the shadow of death,
>   I fear no evil;
> for thou art with me;
>   thy rod and thy staff,
>   they comfort me.
>
> 5 Thou preparest a table before me
>   in the presence of my enemies;
> thou anointest my head with oil,
>   my cup overflows.

---

[3] See L. Sabourin, *The Psalms: Their Origin and Meaning*, 264-265, 320.

[4] See A. Weiser, *The Psalms*, 226-231;   H. –J. Kraus, *Psalmen*, 186-192; A. L. Merrill, "Psalm XXIII and the Jerusalem Tradition," *VT* 15 (1965) 354-360; A. R. Johnson, "Psalm 23 and the Household of Faith," *Proclamation and Presence: Old Testament Essays in Honour of Gwynne Henton Davies* (ed. J. I. Durham & J. R. Porter; Richmond: John Knox, 1970) 255-271; A. von Rohr Sauer, "Fact and Image in the Shepherd Psalm," *CTM* 42 (1971) 488-492; P. Milne, "Psalm 23: Echoes of the Exodus," *Studies in Religion/Sciences religieuses* 4 (1974-75) 237-247; S. Terrien, *The Elusive Presence*, 332-336.

> [6]Surely goodness and mercy shall follow me
>   all the days of my life;
> and I shall dwell in the house of the Lord
>   for ever.

For many people this is the best known and most utilized psalm in the entire Psalter. Its universal appeal stems from its combination of simplicity and richness. Most likely it contains two images: shepherd (vv 1-4) and host (vv 5-6). However, as B. W. Anderson points out,[5] both images are set against the background of the desert. The protector of the sheep is also the protector of the traveller who provides hospitality in his tent as well as protection from all the enemies of the desert. To know such a shepherd-host is to know security.

The term "shepherd" also has political overtones which heighten the sense of protection and equilibrium. In the ancient Near East kings were commonly called shepherds. This implied that they attained their proper identity by meeting the needs of their people. "Shepherd" means, therefore, total concern for and dedication to others (see Isa 40:11; Jer 23:1; Ezek 34:1-31).[6] Here the psalmist links the connotation of shepherd with the dynamism of Yahweh's name. According to verse 3 Yahweh leads for the honor of his name. Fidelity to his name and hence fidelity to his covenant commitment provokes Yahweh to take more than a passing interest in his sheep.

By selecting a few concrete verbs, the psalmist evokes the whole character of pastoral concern ("lie down," "lead," "comfort").[7] Pastures and waters (v 2) reveal Yahweh as provider, leader, and sustainer. The rod (v 4) is a defensive weapon against wild animals. The staff (v 4) is a supportive instrument for the shepherd as he patiently urges on the

---

[5] B. W. Anderson, *Out of the Depths*, 145-146.
[6] See J. Jeremias, "*poimēn* ktl.," *TDNT* 6, 485-502.
[7] See L. Alonso Schökel, *Treinta Salmos*, 113.

grazing sheep. On occasion the shepherd will employ both rod and staff against the lagging or straying sheep. Hence both the rod and the staff are symbols of concern and dedication. We are not surprised, therefore, that the sheep are without fear (v 4).

There is a contrast in the host image but one which complements the shepherd image. Here Yahweh performs all the amenities of a host: spreading the table and anointing the head (v 5). Significantly these actions occur " in the presence of my enemies" (v 5). It is tempting to see these enemies as the former opponents of the psalmist. In this case the enemies witness the reversal that has taken place. Instead of being harassed, the guest of Yahweh enjoys all the comforts of desert hospitality.[8] For the enemies this is indeed the agony of defeat.

"Goodness and mercy"(v 6) is an expression that captures the implications of covenant commitment. "Mercy" (*ḥesed* in Hebrew) connotes Yahweh's abiding fidelity because of his covenant relationship. It is the assurance that God's willingness to provide will be demonstrated in a concrete way.[9] "Goodness" conjures up the dimensions of friendship and good relations that flow from the covenant bond.[10] Although this protestation of divine provision occurs in Yahweh's house, this need not mean that the psalmist is a cultic employee in the temple. It may simply be interpreted as the ongoing assurance of Yahweh's presence.

[8] E. Vogt ("The 'Place in Life' of Psalm 23," *Biblica* 34 [1953] 195-211) thinks that this psalm is to be linked with a thanksgiving sacrifice which a pilgrim offered after he had been unjustly accused and then acquitted.

[9] See K. Doob Sakenfeld, *The Meaning of Hesed in the Hebrew Bible: A New Inquiry* (Harvard Semitic Monographs 17; Missoula, Montana: Scholars Press, 1978).

[10] See W. L. Moran, "A Note on the Treaty Terminology of the Sefire Stelas," *Journal of Near Eastern Studies* 22 (1963) 173-176; D. R. Hillers, "A Note on Some Treaty Terminology in the Old Testament," *BASOR* 176 (1964) 46-47; M. Fox, *ṭôb* as Covenant Terminology," *BASOR* 209 (1973) 41-42; I. Johag, "*ṭôb*. Terminus technicus in Vertrags-und Bundnisformularen des Alten Orients und des Alten Testaments," *Bausteine Biblischer Theologie: Festgabe für G. Johannes Botterweck* (ed. H.-J. Fabry; Bonner Biblische Beiträge 50; Cologne/Bonn: Hanstein, 1977) 3-23.

We are not surprised that Psalm 23 finds a conspicuous place in funeral celebrations. On such occasions we pray for the comfort of the deceased and for his or her abiding place with our God. In so doing we express all those dimensions of harmony and unruffledness which are so typical of the psalms of trust or confidence. It is a peace that is remote from our technology and our business practices.

Covenant, however, is a two-edged sword. It challenges us in this instance not only to experience our own personal harmony and rootedness in God but also to reach out and be the catalysts of trust and hope for others. To be in covenant with this God means to sustain this God's people. In the analogy of the funeral we must employ Psalm 23 not only for the deceased but also for the bereaved. "To prepare the table" (v 5) means more than providing a meal after the burial. "To lie down in green pastures" (v 2) implies more than attending the wake. In our communings with our God we are urged to share our harmony and peace with others. Ours is not the task to explain the mystery of death and theologize about divine retribution.[11] In genuine prayer which breaks free of the prie-dieu and invades the world, ours is the duty to be a staff for others to lean on and a rod to move on gently with the sorrowing.[12] Our bold reliance on our covenant God and our sense of ease in his presence imply that we make our prayer actively contagious for the less than courageous and those ill at ease.

[11] See N. C. Habel, "'Only the Jackal Is My Friend.' On Friends and Redeemers in Job," *Int* 31 (1977) 227-236, esp. 236.

[12] A. Heschel (*Man's Quest for God*, 94) writes: "After prayer we know that prayer is a privilege, to be earned through existence. To pray what we sense, we must live what we pray . . . . Our problem is how to live what we pray, how to make our lives a daily commentary on our prayer book, how to live in consonance with what we promise, how to keep faith with the vision we pronounce."

Psalm 11[13]

In the LORD I take refuge;
how can you say to me,
"Flee like a bird to the mountains;
[2]for lo, the wicked bend the bow,
   they have fitted their arrow to the string,
   to shoot in the dark at the upright in heart;
[3]if the foundations are destroyed,
   what can the righteous do?"
[4]The LORD is in his holy temple,
   the LORD's throne is in heaven;
   his eyes behold, his eyelids test,
   the children of men.
[5]The LORD tests the righteous and the wicked,
   and his soul hates him that loves violence.
[6]On the wicked he will rain coals of
   fire and brimstone;
   a scorching wind shall be the portion of their cup.
[7]For the LORD is righteous, he loves
   righteous deeds;
   the upright shall behold his face.

Our human experience attests that injustice flourishes and that the violence done to the poor is frequently not redressed. We also know that corruption even invades our courts and seduces our judicial personnel. Not even our supreme courts are the ultimate bastions for dispensing justice to all. Perhaps without articulating it, we raise the following question deep within our anguished spirit: is there any final source that will mete out justice to the wronged and punishment to the guilty?

According to L. Alonso Schökel the setting of this psalm is the temple. A persecuted innocent man flees to

---

[13]See A. Weiser, *The Psalms*, 154-158; H. –J. Kraus, *Psalmen*, 88-92.
[14]L. Alonso Schökel, *Treinta Salmos*, 83.

God's house and invokes the right of asylum.[15] The temple employees inform him that the temple does not provide absolutely certain asylum. They advise him, therefore, to flee to the mountains like a bird (v 1). He reacts to such advice by professing his unshakeable confidence in the judgment of Yahweh (vv 4-7). When the foundations of public order are overthrown (v 3), the ultimate hope of justice resides with Yahweh.

The author sets up a dialectic between Yahweh and the persecuted innocent man.[16] According to verse 7 Yahweh is righteous and in verse 5 Yahweh tests the righteous,[17] hence the psalmist. There is another dialectic between light and darkness. In verse 2 the wicked shoot in the dark at the just man. However, according to verse 4 God's eyes pierce the darkness, exposing everyone and everything. Finally there is a dialectic with regard to the punishment. In verse 2 the wicked bend the bow and shoot their arrow. But in verse 6 Yahweh reaches into his own arsenal to mete out justice: fiery coals, brimstone, burning blast.

The divine throne, the mountains, and the temple develop the psalmist's views of presence and concomitant security. God's throne (v 4) is a law tribunal. The heavens (v 4) show that this throne is the supreme court where Yahweh examines all humans without distinction (vv 4-5). In turn, what makes the temple secure is the presence of Yahweh. The mountains (v 1) enter this paradigm of refuge in order to be

[15] See R. de Vaux, *Ancient Israel: Its Life and Institutions* (New York: McGraw-Hill, 1961) 276, 414.

[16] See L. Alonso Schökel, *Treinta Salmos*, 83.

[17] The Hebrew word underlying the translation "righteous" has to do with both divine and human behavior (see previously in Ps 23:3). It implies that behavior which is consonant with the covenant relationship. It is a reality not measurable by any objective intellectual norm. Hence it is a reality which demonstrates through concrete actions that the covenant partners take each other seriously. See G. von Rad, *Old Testament Theology* (New York: Harper & Row, 1962), 1. 370-383; "'Righteousness' and 'Life' in the Cultic Language of the Psalms," *The Problem of the Hexateuch and Other Essays* (New York: McGraw-Hill, 1966) 243-266. For the gracious initiative of God in this relationship see H. H. Guthrie, *Theology as Thanksgiving*, 9.

rejected.[18] It is only Yahweh who is the final source of genuine security. In the end the just person realizes that injustice and violence[19] will not be the last word. There is always Yahweh, the ultimate court of appeal. Though human courts may fail, this final court of appeal in heaven is totally reliable and dependable.

At prayer we enjoy our own legal system where the Lawyer does not ask: "can you pay?" but "in what way may I serve you?" This realization affords security and confidence. In the presence of this God there is no question of wiretapping or phone bugging. Ours is a God who knows the situation even before we attempt to explicate it to ourselves. Ultimately our sense of redress and administration of justice does not reside in a system but in a person. At prayer we are not involved in legal maneuvers but with a Thou who soothes the pain of rejection and the ignominy of ostracism. This is indeed the sufficient God.[20] We do not lick our wounds. Rather, there is Another who binds them up, pouring in oil and wine (Luke 10:34).

Like Psalm 23, this psalm must help us not merely to find security with Another but to be security for others. The God who pampers us in his sanctuary is also the God who empowers us in the marketplace. We simply cannot look on complacently when the foundations of justice are overthrown and people, especially the poor, are the victims.[21] At

[18] See L. Alonso Schökel, *Treinta Salmos*, 84-85.

[19] The word "violence" (in Hebrew *ḥāmās*) is very much at home in the prophetic literature. It expresses arbitrary oppression and inconsiderate domination of fellow humans by the one wielding power. See N. Lohfink, "The Sin of All Mankind and the Sin of the Elect, according to the Priestly Document," *Great Themes from the Old Testament* (Chicago: Franciscan Herald Press, 1981) 229-231. For the centrality and significance of power as a theme of Old Testament research see N. Lohfink, "'Gewalt' als Thema alttestamentlicher Forschung," *Gewalt und Gewaltlosigkeit im Alten Testament* (ed. N. Lohfink; Quaestiones Disputatae 96; Freiburg: Herder, 1983) 15-50.

[20] See S. Terrien, *The Elusive Presence*, 332, 348 #149.

[21] For Yahweh's intervention in the Exodus to create a world of justice see J. P. Miranda, *Marx and the Bible: A Critique of the Philosophy of Oppression* (Maryknoll, New York: Orbis, 1974) 77-108; J. S. Croatto, *Exodus: A Hermeneutics of Freedom* (Maryknoll, New York: Orbis, 1981) 12-30.

prayer we are challenged to denounce all those "systems"
that choose to remain anonymous so that the suffering may
bring no charges against them. To be in covenant means to
sustain the weakest in covenant. Genuine justice is in session
with Yahweh presiding, only when the reciters of Psalm 11
translate their experience of exoneration into meaningful
action for all those denied their rights. Because of covenant
our prayer necessarily has community overtones.[22]

Psalm 91[23]

> He who dwells in the shelter of the Most High,
> who abides in the shadow of the Almighty,
> [2]will say to the LORD, "My refuge and my
> fortress;
> my God, in whom I trust."
> [3]For he will deliver you from the snare
> of the fowler and from the deadly pestilence;
> [4]he will cover you with his pinions,
> and under his wings you will find refuge;
> his faithfulness is a shield and buckler.
> [5]You will not fear the terror of the night,
> nor the arrow that flies by day,
> [6]nor the pestilence that stalks in darkness,
> nor the destruction that wastes at noonday,
> [7]A thousand may fall at your side,
> ten thousand at your right hand;
> but it will not come near you.
> [8]You will only look with your eyes
> and see the recompense of the wicked.
>
> [9]Because you have made the LORD your refuge,
> the Most High your habitation,

---

[22]For the prophetic role of dispensing justice see J. F. Craghan, "The Priest as
Prophet," *Emmanuel* 86 (1980) 639-648.

[23]See A. Weiser, *The Psalms*, 603-613;   H. - J. Kraus, *Psalmen*, 634-640; P.
Hugger, *Jahwe meine Zuflucht: Gestalt und Theologie des 91. Psalms* (Mün-
sterschwarzacher Studien 13; Münsterschwarzach: Vier-Türme Verlag, 1971).

[10]no evil shall befall you,
no scourge come near your tent.
[11]For he will give his angels charge of you
to guard you in all your ways.
[12]On their hands they will bear you up,
lest you dash your foot against a stone.
[13]You will tread on the lion and the adder,
the young lion and the serpent
you will trample under foot.
[14]Because he cleaves to me in love, I
will deliver him;
I will protect him, because he
knows my name.
[15]When he calls to me, I will answer him;
I will be with him in trouble,
I will rescue him and honor him.
[16]With long life I will satisfy him,
and show him my salvation.

How will Yahweh intervene on my behalf? Specifically, what kind of protection will he grant me? In answer to these questions Psalm 91 uses a variety of images to concretize the manner and the kind of divine intervention and protection. It may be divided as follows: (a) an introduction (vv 1-2) which welcomes the pilgrim to the sanctuary (verse 2b was possibly recited by the pilgrim[24]); (b) a priestly sermonette of encouragement (vv 3-13) given in the sanctuary; (c) a final oracle (vv 14-16) spoken in God's name.[25]

According to verses 3-4 intervention means release from the fowler's trap and immunization against a devastating pestilence. Yahweh is described as a mighty bird who takes the psalmist under his wing (see Ex 19:4; Deut 32:11). However, Yahweh is also a mighty warrior. His fidelity takes the form of standard military hardware (v 4b). In

[24]See C. Stuhlmueller, *Psalms* 2. 73.
[25]See R. E. Murphy, "Psalms," *JBC* 35:107, p. 592.

terms of dangers verses 5-6 spell out four crises for four periods of time: (a) terror of the night; (b) arrow of the day; (c) pestilence at evening, i.e., "darkness"; (4) the devastating plague at noon. God's presence means the absence of fear in the face of such formidable dangers. It is interesting to note that the psalmist balances these four temporal crises with four animals in verse 13: (a) lion; (b) adder; (c) young lion; (d) serpent.[26]

Other images of divine protection and a statement of divine retribution unfold in verses 7-12. The psalmist develops the pestilence of verse 3. According to verse 7, though innumerable people fall victim to the rampaging disease, the one trusting in Yahweh has no reason to fear. Verses 8-10 contain a statement of the traditional belief in retribution, viz., during life the just will be vindicated for their loyalty while the wicked will certainly be punished. (This theology holds true only for people in orientation — the experience of disorientation more than questions its validity.) Finally in verses 11-12 the company of angels[27] offers safety on the rocky roads of the Near East.[28]

The psalm comes to a conclusion in verses 14-16 which many take to be a divine oracle spoken by a priest or some other official. Whether or not a cultic intervention is posited, what is clear is that these verses articulate the theology of the psalm, viz., fidelity to Yahweh means deliverance from any and all forms of distress. "Salvation" (v 16) is the concrete this-worldly demonstration of divine concern and compassion. In this psalm confidence presupposes a black and white world where injustice is redressed with mathematical precision. This is indeed a world of order and equilibrium.

---

[26] For the psalmist's use of the ancient Near Eastern myth of slaying the dragon see A. Weiser, *The Psalms*, 611-612.

[27] See V. Hirth, *Gottes Boten im Alten Testament* (Theologische Arbeiten 32; Berlin: Evangelische Verlagsanstalt, 1975) 67-74.

[28] For Q's use of Psalm 91 in the temptation account of Matthew and Luke see H. H. Guthrie, *Theology as Thanksgiving*, 156-157.

At prayer the imagery of this psalm must provoke a reaction. As the psalm develops, we perceive a variety of images, all calculated to conjure up security and protection, for example, the fowler (v 3), the giant bird (v 4), the mighty warrior (v 4), the provider of heavenly company (v 11). Perhaps we would be constrained to understand our God after the manner of Fort Knox, nuclear warfare, or the Pentagon. But putting aside our constraints, we are invited to test the theology of the biblical imagery and make it the springboard for our prayer, or at least certain dimensions of our prayer. In speaking of the psalms and their contribution to biblical education, W. Brueggemann offers this advice in appropriating the symbolic value of these compositions: "This may be the most urgent educational task facing the church — to enable persons to accept life and vocation as being grounded in another whose name and purpose we know."[29]

Psalm 121[30]

> I lift up my eyes to the hills.
>> From whence does my help come?
> [2]My help comes from the LORD
>> who made heaven and earth.
>
> [3]He will not let your foot be moved,
>> he who keeps you will not slumber.
> [4]Behold, he who keeps Israel
>> will neither slumber nor sleep.
> [5]The LORD is your keeper;
>> the LORD is your shade on your right hand.
> [6]The sun shall not smite you by day,
>> nor the moon by night.
>
> [7]The LORD will keep you from all evil;
>> he will keep your life.

---

[29] W. Brueggemann, *The Creative Word*, 94.
[30] See A. Weiser, *The Psalms*, 744-749; H. –J. Kraus, *Psalmen*, 833-837.

[8]The LORD will keep your going out and your coming in
from this time forth and for evermore.

Psalms 120-134 are a special collection in the Psalter.[31]
They are called songs of ascent because of their use as
pilgrim psalms, i.e., pilgrims employed these psalms as they
went up or "ascended" to Jerusalem. Although this collection consists of different literary types, it does contain certain common features. "Joyful confidence in God, hopeful
requests of forgiveness, expressions of thanksgiving for the
Lord's kindness towards Israel, . . . feature among the main
thoughts voiced in these psalms . . ."[32] In these psalms the
poet takes a simple idea, a literary motif, an image and then
develops it with an economy of words. These psalms do not
intend to inculcate an idea. Rather, they are lyrical, seeking
to penetrate sweetly.[33]
    Alonso Schökel suggests that the image or motif here is
the keeper or guardian.[34] Indeed the root "keep" is repeated
six times (vv 3,4,5,7 [2x],8). In developing this image or
motif, the psalmist intersperses possible dangers. In verse 3
there is the danger of one's foot slipping or Yahweh's slum-
bering. In verse 6 there is the danger of exposure to the
dangerous Palestinian sun as well as the danger of the
superstitious power of the moon. However, all these
dangers are offset by the recurring image or motif, viz., the
guardian or keeper.

---

[31]See C. C. Keet, *A Study of the Psalms of Ascent* (London: Mitre, 1969). On
this topic K. Seybold (*Die Wallfahrtspsalmen: Studien zur Entstehungsgeschichte
von Psalm 120-134* [*Biblisch-Theologische Studien 3; Neukirchen-Vluyn: Neukirchener Verlag, 1978*]; "Die Redaktion der Wallfahrtspsalmen," *ZAW* 97 [1979]
247-268) has seen in their final redaction a prayer book for pilgrims in the
postexilic period. H. Seidel ("Wallfahrtslieder," *Das Lebendige Wort: Festgabe
für Gottfriend Voigt* ed. H. Seidel & K.-H. Bieritz; Berlin: Evangelische Verlagsanstalt, 1982] 26-40) situates these psalms in the Levitical preaching between
515-400 B. C., observing that they reflect in a meditative way upon the meaning of
past events.

[32]L. Sabourin, *The Psalms: Their Origin and Meaning*, 11.

[33]See L. Alonso Schökel, *Treinta Salmos*, 344.

[34]Ibid., 345.

Concerning the scene one must note that after the first person in verses 1-2 the third person appears in verse 3. Since no particular scene is described, authors have made several suggestions, e.g., a lonely sentinel making his rounds, an insomniac, a person seeking help. Dismissing these suggestions, Alonso Schökel recommends the silence and the solitude of the night as the scene.[35]

A man raises his eyes from the city and its walls to the natural defense of the surrounding mountains. His glance continues to the top of the mountain and reaches the heavens (v 1). His thoughts are now on Yahweh who made heaven and earth (v 2). The man's glance has been the interrogator and now, having arrived at the heavens, receives a totally satisfying answer (vv 3-8). The one at prayer has answered his own question, realizing that Another guarantees that answer. That answer is basically a theology of concern. It is the assurance that the omnipotent Creator of heaven and earth looks to the needs of one frail human being. Confidence consists in knowing that one is not a nameless face in a chaos of anonymity. There is a God who does care.[36]

Pursuing this impression of confidence, Alonso Schökel finds its prolongation in a night scene where a mother cradles her child to sleep. The back and forth motion of the rocking lulls the child to sleep. Clearly there is no need for fear since the child senses the presence of its mother. Aware that its mother is watching and not dozing, the child can enjoy the rocking, close its eyes, and fall peacefully asleep.[37]

At prayer we are asked to focus on the goodness of Another. While not dismissing our problems, we are urged to concentrate on One who gives and provides because that is the nature of this God. In the wake of the explosion of thing-oriented technology we are invited to delight in Another who accepts us with our limitations and our fears. The image of Mother Yahweh comes immediately to

---

[35] Ibid.   [36] Ibid.   [37] Ibid., 347-348.

mind.[38] This is the God who nurses and sustains us without tabulating the cost because mothers do not enter energy expenses into computers. This is the God who protects and shelters us without calculating the risks because mothers do not operate on a "do ut des" basis. At prayer, therefore, we are to find delight and happiness. After such an experience we can return to our world with renewed energy and zest because of the conviction that Another cares, especially through other covenant partners.

In the setting of covenant we are also to recall the many others in our lives who exercise the ministry of caring for us. We are to remember those people who represented Mother Yahweh when we were ill, when we were depressed, when we were down and out. But recollection must bear fruit in our pursuing the office of Mother Yahweh for others. We are bidden to be keeper and guardian for those who make up the fabric of our lives. In this way our own experience of tranquillity and security becomes the catalyst for meeting the needs of others. Hence while we fall peacefully asleep in the arms of Mother Yahweh, we are also awake to the call for help coming from Mother Yahweh's other children.

Psalm 62[39]

For God alone my soul waits in silence;
    from him comes my salvation.
[2]He only is my rock and my salvation,
    my fortress; I shall not be greatly moved.
[3]How long will you set upon a man
    to shatter him, all of you,
    like a leaning wall, a tottering fence?
[4]They only plan to thrust him down
    from his eminence.

[38]See P. Trible, "God, Nature of," *IDBSup*, 368-369; *God and the Rhetoric of Sexuality* (Overtures to Biblical Theology; Philadelphia: Fortress, 1978) 1-71. For the covenant implications of the sexual imagery see W. Brueggemann, "Israel's Social Criticism and Yahweh's Sexuality," *JAAR* 45 (1977) 739-772.

[39]See A. Weiser, *The Psalms*, 445-453; H. – J. Kraus, *Psalmen*, 435-439.

They take pleasure in falsehood.
They bless with their mouths,
  but inwardly they curse.
5For God alone my soul waits in silence,
  for my hope is from him.
6He only is my rock and my salvation,
  my fortress; I shall not be shaken.
7On God rests my deliverance and my honor;
  my mighty rock, my refuge is God.

8Trust in him at all times, O people;
  pour out your heart before him;
  God is a refuge for us.

9Men of low estate are but a breath,
  men of high estate are a delusion;
 in the balances they go up;
  they are together lighter than a breath.
10Put no confidence in extortion,
  set no vain hopes on robbery;
  if riches increase, set not your heart on them.

11Once God has spoken;
  twice have I heard this:
 that power belongs to God;
12and that to thee, O Lord, belongs
  steadfast love.
 For thou dost requite a man
  according to his work.

Will my real friends please stand up? Will my real values
kindly make themselves known? Is there anyone who will
prove to be totally reliable? These are the implicit questions
which this psalm poses in its own meditative way. Like
Psalm 121, this poem does not speak *to* God but *about* God
(with the exception of verse 12). It challenges the person at
prayer to entertain questions about genuine values.

The psalm opens with an introduction about Yahweh (vv

1-2). This then leads to the critique of values in verses 3-10. Trust in God (vv 5-8) is bracketed by false friends/values (vv3-4) and human weakness (vv 9-10). The psalm concludes with a statement of Yahweh's covenantal fidelity (vv 11-12a) and a later addition in the style of the wisdom tradition (v12b).

For the psalmist Yahweh is the bastion of security who offers him ("soul" in verse 1 is the total conscious self) victory or salvation. This security is reflected in the images of rock and fortress which lead to the conviction of unshakableness (v 2). What is significant is that only God (v 2; see "God alone" in verse 1) provides such reliability or certainty. The psalmist next reflects on his false friends by way of contrast. They oppress him (v 3), intending only to bring about his destruction. Lies have become their way of life. They say one thing (blessing) but mean another (curse — v 4). Again the refrain appears (vv 5-6): only God is the really dependable one. Hope resides in him alone.[40]

In verse 7 the psalmist adds to the earlier images of security: honor (= heaviness, hence reliable) and refuge. Turning now to the assembly, the psalmist lets his experience have an impact on them. Only God (v 8) is deserving of trust. On the other hand, all humans — both great and small — lack the stability of Yahweh (v 9). The following, therefore, are not lasting values: extortion, robbery, increased wealth (v 10). In the conclusion the psalmist insists that genuine power belongs to God (v 11). Moreover, Yahweh is a practitioner of covenant values ("steadfast love" in verse 12a). According to the addition, therefore, Yahweh treats humans justly (v 12b).

At prayer we raise the question of values. Without disparaging all humans, we realize that in not a few instances power is the name of the game. Wealth, prestige, position —

[40] See A. Deissler, "Das Israel der Psalmen als Gottesvolk der Hoffenden," *Die Zeit Jesu: Festschrift für Heinrich Schlier* (ed. G. Bornkamm & K. Rahner; Freiburg: Herder, 1970) 15-37.

to name only a few — are manifestations of power. According to Paul they are forms of that uncontrollable power unleashed upon the world since the time of the first sin.[41] Such forms pervert and manipulate, trying to suck humans down the vortex of their insatiable desires. The disillusion is that they are never totally satisfying. In one direction prayer forces us to assess our contribution to this power by our own sinfulness.[42] In another direction prayer compels us to place our values in persons: in our God and in other humans to the extent that they are open to the good of others. Humans, after all, must be rock and refuge for other humans. In that way they share their own stability and dependability, reflecting the solidity of the Rock.

New Testament

Matthew 6:25-30

[25]"Therefore I tell you, do not be anxious about your life, what you shall eat or what you shall drink, nor about your body, what you shall put on. Is not life more than food, and the body more than clothing?[26] Look at the birds of the air: they neither sow nor reap nor gather into barns, and yet your heavenly Father feeds them. Are you not of more value than they?[27] And which of you by being anxious can add one cubit to his span of life?[28] And why are you anxious about clothing? Consider the lilies of the field, how they grow; they neither toil nor spin; [29]yet I tell you, even Solomon in all his glory was not arrayed like one of these.[30] But if God so clothes the grass of the field, which today is alive and tomorrow is thrown into the oven, will he not much more clothe you, O men of little faith?

[41] See J. Murphy-O'Connor, *Becoming Human Together: The Pastoral Anthropology* (2d ed; Good News Studies 2; Wilmington: Michael Glazier, 1982) 89-105.

[42] See S. Lyonnet, "Original Sin and Romans 5:12-14," *Theology Digest* 5 (1957) 54-57, esp. 54.

In this section of his Sermon on the Mount Matthew calls upon his community to extricate itself from anxieties about daily needs (v 25). Although this is not a psalm of trust or confidence, it reflects many of the characteristics of this psalm type. In both biblical traditions it is not a question of flight from concern about these real needs. Rather, the focus is on "'anxiety' which expresses total absorption in the goods of this world. Discipleship frees one to trust in the only true Giver and Sustainer of life."[43] In verses 26-29 Matthew presents examples confirming the Father's unrelenting care of the disciples. The Father feeds the birds and decks the lilies of the field with a purple more resplendent than Solomon's royal robes. If, therefore, the Father devotes such attention to this passing world, will he not take greater care of his own family (v 30)?

In the spirit of the psalms of trust or confidence Matthew hammers home the truth that we must run the risk of grounding ourselves in Another. By taking such a risk, we open ourselves to the realization that our God is genuinely interested in us as persons and that commitment to his pledged word means ongoing concern. Harmony and stability, therefore, do not result from a flight from the legitimate concerns of everyday life but from a concentration on the character of our God — the Giver par excellence (see also Matt 11:28-30).

In another passage Matthew exposes the covenant dimension of this trust or confidence, viz., concern for others. In the great scene of the last judgment (Matt 25:31-46) Matthew expounds the doctrine of harmony and contentment at that judgment by focusing on the person of Jesus. "'Truly, I say to you, as you did it to one of the least of these my brethren, you did it to me'" (v 40). For Matthew Jesus is reflected in the hungry, the thirsty, the stranger, the naked, the sick, and the imprisoned. "These deeds for others

---

[43] J. P. Meier, *Matthew* (New Testament Message: Wilmington: Michael Glazier, 1980) 66.

are the criterion of judgment because they define a person's essential behavior and relation to the Judge, not just to other men."[44] To be rooted in our God, to experience consolation and contentment means to mediate to fellow humans our experience of consolation and contentment. To know this God is to know this God's extended family.

Summary of the theology of the psalms of trust or confidence [45]

> (1) While life does have its problems, frustrations, and agonies, life also attests to a covenant God who inspires confidence in the midst of these concerns.
>
> (2) To pray these psalms to our covenant God also means to pray them for his covenant people, i.e., all those who do not experience harmony and equilibrium. Such prayer must be action-oriented.
>
> (3) It is not without significance that our ability to trust often emerges after the experience of pain and anxiety.
>
> (4) These psalms presuppose a sense of true values. To be hooked on the human quest for power is to destroy the equilibrium and balance assumed by these psalms.
>
> (5) These psalms are the radical ability to recall our history with our God and to live trusting lives on the basis of that history.

[44] Ibid., 304.

[45] Other psalms of trust or confidence include the following: 16, 125, 131.

4

To the Good Life
The Wisdom Psalms

Living versus existing

Should we merely exist in the expectation of a blessed eternity or dare we live for the sheer joy of living? Is life a burden to be borne with stiff upper lip tenacity or is it a gift to be shared with others in community? Is life merely a passage or is it a series of grace-filled moments? Is life to be tolerated or to be lived? Is life to be cursed or to be blessed?

With our great preoccupation with the heaven symbol we have been indoctrinated to be dropouts from life.[1] Living thus becomes the condition for the hereafter where accounts will be settled and "genuine" living will begin. We have been taught to put up with life, to make deals with life, so that we may get on with the real business of preparing for eternal bliss. The heaven symbol has often cheated us out of the possibility of living and thereby out of the opportunity to acknowledge the Living One as the giver of gifts. With an overemphasis on the beatific vision we can no longer see beatific humans and their gifts.

By and large Israel's wisdom writers, e.g., the authors of Job, Proverbs, and Ecclesiastes, did not accept an afterlife.[2] Their great contribution was to look at life and assess what

---

[1] See W. Brueggemann, "Scripture and an Ecumenical Life-Style: A Study in Wisdom Theology," *Int* 24 (1970) 3-19, esp. 12-14.

[2] In the deuterocanonical works two wisdom authors are significant for their different views about an afterlife. See A. A. Di Lella, "Conservative and Progres-

made for living and what did not. Wisdom was, therefore, the art of steering a course through life,[3] observing both the pluses and minuses. The whole outlook of these writers was based on the gift of creation. In their view God created responsible humans who were to care for his/their world, not puppets who would irrationally react to the tug of the puppeteer's string.[4] For these writers humans were charged with the sacred task of transforming his/their world — they were to relish life because the Creator had proclaimed that it was good, very good.

At prayer we experience the goodness of our God. Our prayers, however, are not to be computer readouts of the qualities of our God. They are not to be layaways for real life later on. At prayer we realize that God is the giver of gifts and that to acknowledge the gift in whatever form is to acknowledge the Giver. This does not mean that we fail to see the absence of gifts in so many quarters of our world. Rather, it means that we see the good life as grace for all, not

sive Theology: Sirach and Wisdom," *CBQ* 28 (1966) 139-154, esp. 143-146, 154. The consensus of scholars has been that no hope of survival after death is expressed in the Old Testament prior to the second century B. C. One of the greatest opponents of this consensus has been M. Dahood who argued that the psalms say a great deal about immortality and resurrection (see *Psalms* [3 vols.; AB 16; Garden City, New York: Doubleday, 1966-1970] under "afterlife" and immortality"). Recent scholarly writing has indicated that these two positions must be greatly nuanced. A sampling of such writing would include the following: A. — M. Dubarle, "Belief in Immortality in the Old Testament and Judaism," *Immortality and Resurrection* (ed. P. Benoit et al.; Concilium 60; New York: Herder & Herder, 1970) 34-45; G. E. W. Nickelsburg, *Resurrection, Immortality, and Eternal Life in Intertestamental Judaism* (Harvard Theological Studies; Cambridge: Harvard University, 1972); B. Vawter, "Intimations of Immortality and the Old Testament," *JBL* 91 (1972) 158-171; H. C. Brichto, "Kin, Cult, Land and Afterlife," *Hebrew Union College Annual* 44 (1973) 1-54; J. F. A. Sawyer, "Hebrew Words for the Resurrection of the Dead," *VT* 23 (1973) 218-234; J. J. Collins, "Apocalyptic Eschatology as the Transcendence of Death," *CBQ* 36 (1974) 21-43; G. W. Coats, "Death and Dying in Old Testament Tradition," *Lexington Theological Quarterly* 2 (1976) 9-14; L. R. Bailey, *Biblical Perspectives on Death* (Philadelphia: Fortress, 1979).

[3] See W. Zimmerli, "Concerning the Structure of Old Testament Wisdom," *Studies in Ancient Israelite Wisdom*, 177-207.

[4] For the influence of wisdom on the other sections of the Old Testament canon see D. F. Morgan, *Wisdom in the Old Testament Traditions* (Atlanta: John Knox, 1981).

hoarded treasures for only a few.[5] Stability and harmony are to be the patrimony of all.

Wisdom psalms

Wisdom psalms are not as apparent as, for example, the psalms of descriptive praise or the psalms of declarative praise. It is not surprising, therefore, that there is no little debate on the number of psalms belonging to this category.[6] However, on the basis of stylistic and linguistic forms as well as themes R. E. Murphy suggests a useful distinction: (a) wisdom psalms that are parallel to other psalm types (Pss 1, 32, 34, 37, 49, 112, 128) and (b) other psalm types that betray wisdom influence (e.g., Pss 25:8-10, 12-14; 31:23-24; 39:4-6).[7] While there is no clear-cut structure in these wisdom psalms properly so-called, there is a common tone inspired by their didactic purposes.

With regard to themes wisdom psalms emphasize the doctrine of retribution, i.e., they attempt to offer a theological explanation of success and failure, reward and punishment.[8] Hence they offer black and white contrasts between the just and the wicked (see Ps 1:4-5). Wisdom psalms are also bent upon providing sound practical advice. They

[5] For the message of wisdom as one of life see R. E. Murphy, "The Kerygma of the Book of Proverbs," *Int* 20 (1966) 3-14.

[6] See S. Mowinckel, "Psalms and Wisdom," *Wisdom in Israel and in the Ancient Near East* (ed. M. Noth & D. W. Thomas; VTSup 3; Leiden: Brill, 1960) 205-224; *The Psalms in Israel's Worship*, 2. 104-114; G. von Rad, *Wisdom in Israel* (New York: Abingdon, 1972) 47-50; J. L. Crenshaw, "Wisdom," *Old Testament Form Criticism*, 247-253; J. K. Kuntz, "The Canonical Wisdom Psalms of Ancient Israel — Their Rhetorical, Thematic, and Formal Dimensions," *Rhetorical Criticism: Essays in Honor of James Muilenburg* (ed. J. J. Jackson & M. Kessler; Pittsburgh Theological Monograph Series 1; Pittsburgh: Pickwick, 1974) 186-222; L. G. Perdue, *Wisdom and Cult* (Society of Biblical Literature Dissertation Series 30; Missoula, Montana: Scholars Press, 1977) 261-343.

[7] R. E. Murphy, "A Consideration of the Classification 'Wisdom Psalms,'" *Congress Volume — Bonn* (VTSup 9; Leiden: Brill, 1962) 159-161.

[8] See J. K. Kuntz, "The Retribution Motif in Psalmic Wisdom," *ZAW* 89 (1977) 223-233.

advocate such virtues as awareness of responsibility, ongoing diligence, etc. (see Ps 37:7-10, 21-22, 34-35). Their hallmark is fear of Yahweh (see Ps 112:1). This is an attitude that is rooted in covenant. To fear Yahweh is to be open to Yahweh's will and world of concerns.[9]

With regard to stylistic and linguistic forms wisdom psalms reflect Israel's traditional way of inculcating morality.[10] They offer comparisons: "Better is a little that the righteous has than the abundance of many wicked" (Ps 37:16). They admonish and advise: "Be not like a horse or mule, without understanding, which must be curbed with bit and bridle, else it will not keep with you" (Ps 32:9). They emphasize good living by way of macarisms or beatitudes: "Blessed is the man to whom the Lord imputes no iniquity" (Ps 32:2). After the manner of the Book of Proverbs (see Prov 1:8,10,15; 2:1, etc.) they depict a father addressing his son: "Come, O sons, listen to me, I will teach you the fear of the Lord" (Ps 34:11).

Psalm 1[11]

> Blessed is the man
> who walks not in the counsel of the wicked,
> nor stands in the way of sinners,
> nor sits in the seat of scoffers;
> [2] but his delight is in the law of the LORD,
> and on his law he meditates day and night.
> [3] He is like a tree
> planted by streams of water,
> that yields its fruit in its season,

[9] See J. Becker, *Gottesfurcht im Alten Testament* (Analecta Biblica 25; Rome: Biblical Institute, 1965); J. Haspecker, *Gottesfurcht bei Jesus Sirach* (Analecta Biblica 30; Rome: Biblical Institute, 1967); L. Derousseaux, *La crainte de Dieu dans l'Ancien Testament* (Lectio Divina 63: Paris: Cerf, 1970).

[10] See R. E. Murphy, *Wisdom Literature* (The Forms of the Old Testament Literature 13; Grand Rapids: Eerdmans, 1981) 47-82.

[11] See A. Weiser, *The Psalms*, 102-108; H. –J. Kraus, *Psalmen*, 1-10.

and its leaf does not wither.
   In all that he does, he prospers.
⁴The wicked are not so,
   but are like chaff which the wind drives away.
⁵Therefore the wicked will not stand in the judgment,
   nor sinners in the congregation of the righteous;
⁶for the LORD knows the way of the righteous,
   but the way of the wicked will perish.

Psalm 1 (together with Psalm 2) is really the introduction to the entire Psalter. Those responsible for this arrangement have made Psalm 1 inculcate an attitude which is to motivate the reading and the praying of the subsequent psalms.[12] As C. Stuhlmueller notes, "Ps 1 was clearly meant to be a coalescing force in the psalter and by its own secular contact to keep the prayer of Israel closely in touch with the total life of Israel and this life closely attached to God."[13] Taken by itself, Psalm 1 may be prayed as a form of orientation but one which challenges the person at prayer to question its black and white picture of reality.

According to L. G. Perdue this psalm is built around the antithetical proverb in verse 6, viz., the contrast between the way of the righteous and the way of the wicked.[14] The psalm begins with a macarism or beatitude in verse 1 ("blessed"). For one author there is a note of envy in the Hebrew word so that it may be translated "that person is to be envied who..."[15] The more common view, however, is that the word simply means "how happy is that person who . . ." It is thus "a congratulatory remark made by an observer as well as the state of blessing into which the decorum of the righteous

[12] See B. S. Childs, *Introduction to the Old Testament as Scripture*, 513-514; C. Westermann, "The Formation of the Psalter," *Praise and Lament*, 253.

[13] C. Stuhlmueller, *Psalms* 1. 59.

[14] L. G. Perdue, *Wisdom and Cult*, 269, 271.

[15] See W. Janzen, "'*Ashrê*' in the Old Testament," *Harvard Theological Review* 58 (1965) 215-226.

man has led him."[16] The psalmist expands the beatitude by dwelling, first of all, on the actions and prosperity of the righteous. Thus he walks, stands, and sits in the right places (v 1).[17] Therefore, he may be likened to a channel-fed tree. No matter what, he always gets ahead (v 3).

The psalmist then develops the proverb in verse 6 by focusing on the wicked. Unlike the righteous, they will not be able to stand (v 5). They are comparable to chaff (v 4), the husks which the wind separates from the grain.

According to Perdue[18] verse 2 is an insertion since it has no parallel in the description of the wicked. On the other hand, this note about meditation on Yahweh's will fills out the picture of the righteous person. Such a person is one who is rooted in a person, Yahweh, and who is then moved to carry out the wise instruction emanating from Yahweh.[19] To separate the person of God from the divine will is always a distortion.

At prayer we may feel inclined to interpret divine retribution in terms of an afterlife. Thus in heaven the righteous will be rewarded while the wicked will be condemned. However, the perspective of the psalmist is this-worldly. Hence retribution takes place in this life. In our now halting effort at prayer we may be able to conjure up some of those genuine people who "made it in this life." Nonetheless we continue to be haunted by the specter of the wicked who also "made it in this life."

Order, normalcy, equilibrium — this is the black and white picture of the psalmist wherein the channel-fed tree and the wind-blown chaff are clearly distinguished. But this

---

[16] L. G. Perdue, *Wisdom and Cult*, 272.

[17] G. André ("'Walk,' 'stand,' and 'sit' in Psalm i 1-2," *VT* 32 1982 327) suggests that the psalmist had Deut 6:4-9 in mind, especially verse 7, in composing this poem — hence total devotion to Yahweh.

[18] L. G. Perdue, *Wisdom and Cult*, 271.

[19] S. Terrien (*The Elusive Presence*, 288) writes: "Response to presence in the awareness of love is the foundation of ethics. Behavior is not motivated by obedience to 'ordinances' and 'statutes.'. . . The will to behave is conditioned by the desire to love."

picture faults our experience. We feel like the author of the poetic dialogues in Job who must challenge the divine judge: "'Oh, that I had one to hear me!'" (Job 31:35). Perhaps the challenge of this psalm is to accept the challenge of mystery.[20] Like Job we are invited, not to turn aside from harsh reality and fail to make our contribution, but to place the demands for order, normalcy, and equilibrium in a Person, not a system. For us this may prove to be the torah or wise instruction of the psalm, i.e., to be in touch with our God, not to be caught up in programs. Thus we are challenged to question the theology of retribution and yet to accept the torah, enigmatic though it may be. At prayer we are in the company of the wise who sought to steer a way through life.

Psalm 128[21]

> Blessed is every one who fears the LORD,
>   who walks in his ways!
> [2]You shall eat the fruit of the labor of your hands;
>   you shall be happy, and it shall be well with you.
> [3]Your wife will be like a fruitful vine
>   within your house;
> your children will be like olive
>   shoots around your table.
> [4]Lo, thus shall the man be blessed
>   who fears the LORD.
>
> [5]The LORD bless you from Zion!
>   May you see the prosperity of Jerusalem
>   all the days of your life!
> [6]May you see your children's children!
>   Peace be upon Israel!

Like Psalm 1, this psalm begins with a beatitude. In this opening verse fearing Yahweh is equated with walking in his

---

[20] For the centrality of mystery in Job see R. A. F. MacKenzie, "The Purpose of the Yahweh Speeches in the Book of Job," *Biblica* 40 (1959) 435-445, esp. 441-444.

[21] See A. Weiser, *The Psalms*, 767-770; H. -J. Kraus, *Psalmen*, 862-864.

ways. After the manner of the Book of Deuteronomy[22] the psalm develops in the following verses the consequences of fearing Yahweh/walking in his ways. According to verse 2 the man will know prosperity, i.e., he will enjoy what he has worked for. According to verse 3 his wife will be fertile and thus he will have a large family. Verse 4 emphasizes this desirable situation by noting the dimension of blessing. Thus to fear Yahweh = to walk in his ways = to be blessed.

As K. Seybold has noted,[23] some psalms of ascent have much in common with the Aaronic blessing (see Num 6:22-26: Ps 67:1) by emphasizing peace and blessings. It is highly significant in this psalm that the blessing of the God-fearing in verses 1-4 is linked to the prosperity of Jerusalem (v 5) and the peace of Israel (v 6). In the psalmist's view the individual and the community are not two isolated entities. They mutually interact so that the success of the one redounds to that of the other. The pilgrim worshiping at the Jerusalem temple is both the member of a people and the head of a local household.

P. D. Miller[24] has studied this temple-home theology and has underlined the dimension of harmony and balance typical of the wisdom psalms. Blessing is, first of all, a bridge which moves from the sanctuary to the ongoing life of the community outside the sanctuary. Second, the frame of reference is divine providence whereby God continues to

---

[22] The Deuteronomic doctrine of retribution may be described as follows. It is the teaching that Yahweh rewards the good that humans do and punishes their evil but only during the course of their earthly existence. For this teaching and its significance see O. S. Rankin, *Israel's Wisdom Literature* (Edinburgh: Clark, 1936; New York: Schocken, 1969) 77-80; A. A. Di Lella, "The Problem of Retribution in the Wisdom Literature," *Rediscovery of Scripture* (Burlington, Wisconsin: Franciscan Educational Conference, 1967) 109-127; J. G. Gammie, "The Theology of Retribution in the Book of Deuteronomy," *CBQ* 32 (1970) 1-12; K. Koch (ed.), *Um das prinzip der Vergeltung in Religion und Recht des Alten Testaments* (Wege der Forschung 125; Darmstadt: Wissenschaftliche Buchgesellschaft, 1972).

[23] K. Seybold, *Der aaronitische Segen: Studien zu Numeri 6,22-27* (Neukirchen-Vluyn: Neukirchener Verlag, 1977) 57-59.

[24] P. D. Miller, "The Blessing of God: An Interpretation of Numbers 6:22-27," *Int* 29 (1975) 240-251.

care for his people. Third, God's blessing is located in the continuity of life, not in a few extraordinary events.[25]

At prayer we are also urged to dwell on the ongoingness of life, not a few extraordinary events. Hence a good job, a good spouse, a lovely family, and the presence of grandchildren make for that wholeness wherein living becomes celebration. To be sure, this psalm does not deal with unemployment, marital crisis, problems in raising children, etc. And yet by reason of blessing itself these issues emerge. To participate in the community's worship is to be involved in the community's destiny. One's personal life is thus bound up with Zion. To acknowledge the harmony and balance in our own lives means to be aware of the disharmony and imbalance in the lives of others. This God always has his family present when we are at the seemingly most intimate moments of our prayer.

Psalm 112[26]

> Praise the LORD.
> Blessed is the man who fears the LORD,
>   who greatly delights in his commandments!
> [2] His descendants will be mighty in the land;
>   the generation of the upright will be blessed.
> [3] Wealth and riches are in his house;
>   and his righteousness endures for ever.
> [4] Light rises in the darkness for the upright;
>   the LORD is gracious, merciful, and righteous.
> [5] It is well with the man who deals
>   generously and lends,
>   who conducts his affairs with justice.
> [6] For the righteous will never be moved;

---

[25] On the theology of blessing see J. Scharbert, "'Fluchen' und 'Segnen' im Alten Testament," *Biblica* 39 (1958) 1-26; "*brk*," *TDOT* 2, 279-308; C. Westermann, *Blessing in the Bible and the Life of the Church* (Overtures to Biblical Theology; Philadelphia: Fortress, 1978) 26-40.

[26] See A. Weiser, *The Psalms*, 702-704; H. –J. Kraus, *Psalmen*, 710-724.

he will be remembered for ever.
⁷He is not afraid of evil tidings;
    his heart is firm, trusting in the LORD.
⁸His heart is steady, he will not be afraid,
    until he sees his desire on his adversaries.

⁹He has distributed freely, he has
    given to the poor;
    his horn is exalted in honor.
¹⁰The wicked man sees it and is angry;
    he gnashes his teeth and melts away;
    the desire of the wicked man comes to nought.

This psalm is an acrostic, i.e., a composition in which the initial letters of sentences or stanzas form a pattern — here the twenty-two letters of the Hebrew alphabet. At the same time, however, the psalmist has artistically constructed a poem which like Psalm 1 contrasts the behavior and fate of the righteous and unrighteous. Like the author of Psalm 1, this poet also begins with a beatitude (v 1) and builds his composition around an antithetical proverb: the righteousness of the just endures forever (vv 3,6,9) while the desire of the wicked is frustrated (v 10).

In verses 2-3 the psalmist notes the blessings of the righteous: prosperity and family. In verses 4-6 he depicts the proper behavior of the righteous: generosity and honest dealings. In verses 7-9 the poet underlines the faith of the righteous: deep trust, fearlessness, generosity to the poor, and honor ("horn" is an image for increased dignity and strength — see Pss 75:10; 89:17,24). Finally in verse 10 the psalmist focuses on the wicked: jealous rage and anger occasioned by the stature and good fortune of the righteous. The psalm closes with a sage remark that the desire of the wicked leads only to frustration.

For the righteous life is indeed worth living. It is a good life replete with family and wealth. It is a life devoid of shocks and preoccupations. It is a life where the good will indeed have the last word. Clearly the basis of this good life is fear of Yahweh and delight in his commandments (v 1). It is an understatement to say that this is a world of harmony and balance.

As in Psalm 1, we are tempted at prayer to shift this world of bliss to the afterlife. However, the only measure of immortality allotted to the righteous is the preservation of their virtue in the ongoing memory of the community. As Perdue notes, " . . . our sagacious author regards himself to be a devotee of the sapiential dogma of retribution, and thus places himself in the company of the pious wise."[27] Still, while our experience conflicts with this theology, we are challenged at prayer to make at least some elements in this theology viable. We are urged to repress evil and to honor virtue in our lives and the lives of our communities. In this way we are called upon to discover the good and unmask the evil. Even though our world will never resemble a perfect world, in prayer we are moved to make it more livable so that the righteous may be duly acknowledged and the wicked exposed and rehabilitated. To contribute a little to the order of our world is to overcome some of its disorder.[28]

Psalm 34[29]

> I will bless the LORD at all times;
>   his praise shall continually be in my mouth.
> [2]My soul makes its boast in the LORD;
>   let the afflicted hear and be glad.
> [3]O magnify the LORD with me,
>   and let us exalt his name together!
> [4]I sought the LORD, and he answered me,
>   and delivered me from all my fears.

[27]L. Perdue, *Wisdom and Cult*, 294.

[28]On the relevance of wisdom as a guide for life's journey and the foundational order of all creation see N. C. Habel, "The Symbolism of Wisdom in Proverbs 1-9," *Int* 26 (1972) 131-157.

[29]See A. Weiser, *The Psalms*, 295-300; H. – J. Kraus, *Psalmen*, 266-272.

⁵Look to him, and be radiant;
    so your faces shall never be ashamed.
⁶This poor man cried, and the LORD heard him,
    and saved him out of all his troubles.
⁷The angel of the LORD encamps
    around those who fear him, and delivers them.
⁸O taste and see that the LORD is good!
    Happy is the man who takes refuge in him!
⁹O fear the LORD, you his saints,
    for those who fear him have no want!
¹⁰The young lions suffer want and hunger;
    but those who seek the LORD lack no good thing.
¹¹Come, O sons, listen to me,
    I will teach you the fear of the LORD,
¹²What man is there who desires life,
    and covets many days, that he may enjoy good?
¹³Keep your tongue from evil,
    and your lips from speaking deceit.
¹⁴Depart from evil, and do good;
    seek peace, and pursue it.

¹⁵The eyes of the LORD are toward the righteous,
    and his ears toward their cry.
¹⁶The face of the LORD is against evildoers,
    to cut off the remembrance of them from the earth.
¹⁷When the righteous cry for help,
    the LORD hears
    and delivers them out of all their troubles.
¹⁸The LORD is near to the brokenhearted,
    and saves the crushed in spirit.

¹⁹Many are the afflictions of the righteous;
    but the LORD delivers him out of them all.
²⁰He keeps all his bones;
    not one of them is broken.
²¹Evil shall slay the wicked;
    and those who hate the righteous
    will be condemned.

[22]The LORD redeems the life of his servants;
    none of those who take refuge in him will be
condemned.

This psalm is also an acrostic, specifically alphabetical.
(The letter *waw* is missing between verses 5 and 6. However,
verse 22 repeats the letter *pe*.[30]) Verses 11-22 are clearly
didactic, dealing with such items as desiring life (v 12) and
avoiding evil/doing good (v 14) and containing the sage's
appeal to sons (v 11). However, verses 1-10 do not seem
initially to be didactic. In an introduction (vv 1-3) the psalmist announces his intention to praise Yahweh, although
noting (v 2) that the afflicted[31] may get a lesson from joining
in. In verses 4-6 the poet seems to be uttering a thanksgiving
or a psalm of declarative praise, describing in general terms
his plight and subsequent deliverance. In verses 7-10 the
poet then develops this experience by exhorting his
audience, among other things, to fear Yahweh (v 9).
Although some authors regard the entire psalm as a thanksgiving or a psalm of declarative praise, Murphy has made a
good case for seeing the thanksgiving element as subservient
to an overall didactic purpose. "But here almost everything
is didactic; the event itself is glossed over and merely serves
as a springboard into wisdom teaching."[32]

In verses 4-10 the psalmist sees his experience, not as an
isolated incident, but as one which necessarily impinges on
the community. The God of Israel is involved in the plight of
individuals. However, the deliverance is reenacted and celebrated so that others may benefit from what would be
otherwise a once and for all happening. In verse 7 the poet
uses the image of Yahweh's messenger ("the angel of the

[30] See P. W. Skehan, "Strophic Patterns in the Book of Job," *CBQ* 23 (1961) 127.

[31] On the problem of the poor and the pious see L. Sabourin, *The Psalms: Their
Origin and Meaning*, 95-98; H. -J. Kraus, *Theologie der Psalmen* (BKAT 15/3;
Neukirchen-Vluyn: Neukirchener Verlag, 1979) 188-193; M. D. Guinan, *Gospel
Poverty: Witness to the Risen Christ* (New York: Paulist, 1981) 45-53, 88-89.

[32] R. E. Murphy, "A Classification," 163.

Lord") —this is basically another form of Yahweh's manifestation whereby the God of the covenant protects his people (see Ex 3:2,4; 14:19-20). Though young lions may go hungry, those who lean on Yahweh do not suffer any want (v 10). Hence the holy people of God[33] are exhorted to fear Yahweh (v 9).

In verses 11-22 the psalmist applies his experience to the needs of his audience. As he sees it, wisdom is a question of desiring life and experiencing the good (v 12). To acquire such gifts, one must control one's speech (v 13) and avoid evil/do good (v 14). By practicing righteousness, the wise integrate themselves into the divinely willed flow of the world. Should they fall into distress, they are able to call upon Yahweh and find relief (vv 17-20). On the other hand, the wicked are necessarily bent upon disrupting the community and causing havoc. It is only fitting that they be removed from the community — hence their memory is obliterated (v 16). Evil will eventually wipe out evil (v 21).

At prayer we must also recall the disruptive experiences in our lives. We are to recollect the times when for one reason or another order gave way to disorder, balance ceded to imbalance, and harmony yielded to disharmony. We are thus bidden to relive a broken world, a world where wisdom is patently lacking, a world where life and peace are but clichés. However, our prayer is not to be an exercise in recalling old falls and catastrophes for memory's sake. Rather, our prayer must make our experience contagious for those who exist but do not live. Prayer must touch the broken community in which we find ourselves so that our experience may be the springboard for hope which is the

---

[33] Here the term "saints" or "holy ones" stands for humans. Usually the term designates members of the heavenly court. See M. Noth, "The Holy Ones of the Most High, "*The Laws in the Pentateuch and Other Studies* (London: Oliver & Boyd, 1966) 215-228, esp. 218. It should be noted that the expression "the people of Yahweh" occurs 354 times while the expression "the people of God" is found only two times. See N. Lohfink, "The People of God," *Grand Themes from the Old Testament*, 117-133.

condition for life. At prayer we are to become the embodiment of: "He keeps all his bones; not one of them is broken" (v 20).

Psalm 37[34]

Fret not yourself because of the wicked,
  be not envious of wrongdoers!
²For they will soon fade like the grass,
  and wither like the green herb.

³Trust in the LORD, and do good;
  so you will dwell in the land, and enjoy security.
⁴Take delight in the LORD,
  and he will give you the desires of your heart.

⁵Commit your way to the LORD;
  trust in him, and he will act.
⁶He will bring forth your vindication as the light,
  and your right as the noonday.
⁷Be still before the LORD, and wait patiently for him;
  fret not yourself over him who
  prospers in his way,
  over the man who carries out evil devices!
⁸Refrain from anger, and forsake wrath!
  Fret not yourself; it tends only to evil.
⁹For the wicked shall be cut off;
  but those who wait for the LORD
  shall possess the land.

¹⁰Yet a little while, and the wicked
  will be no more;
  though you look well at his place,
  he will not be there.
¹¹But the meek shall possess the land,
  and delight themselves in abundant prosperity.

---

[34] See A. Weiser, *The Psalms*, 312-323; H. – J. Kraus, *Psalmen*, 285-292.

¹²The wicked plots against the righteous,
   and gnashes his teeth at him;
¹³but the LORD laughs at the wicked,
   for he sees that his day is coming.
¹⁴The wicked draw the sword and bend their bows,
   to bring down the poor and needy,
   to slay those who walk uprightly;
¹⁵their sword shall enter their own heart,
   and their bows shall be broken.
¹⁶Better is a little that the righteous has
   than the abundance of many wicked.
¹⁷For the arms of the wicked shall be broken;
   but the LORD upholds the righteous.

¹⁸The LORD knows the days of the blameless,
   and their heritage will abide for ever;
¹⁹they are not put to shame in evil times,
   in the days of famine they have abundance.
²⁰But the wicked perish;
   the enemies of the LORD are like the glory of the
   pastures,
   they vanish—like smoke they vanish away.
²¹The wicked borrows, and cannot pay back,
   but the righteous is generous and gives;
²²for those blessed by the LORD shall possess the land,
   but those cursed by him shall be cut off.

²³The steps of a man are from the LORD,
   and he establishes him in whose way he delights;
²⁴though he fall, he shall not be cast headlong,
   for the LORD is the stay of his hand.

²⁵I have been young, and now am old;
   yet I have not seen the righteous forsaken
   or his children begging bread.
²⁶He is ever giving liberally and lending,
   and his children become a blessing.

²⁷Depart from evil, and do good;
   so shall you abide for ever.
²⁸For the LORD loves justice;
   he will not forsake his saints.

The righteous shall be preserved for ever,
   but the children of the wicked shall be cut off.
²⁹The righteous shall possess the land,
   and dwell upon it for ever.

³⁰The mouth of the righteous utters wisdom,
   and his tongue speaks justice.
³¹The law of his God is in his heart;
   his steps do not slip.
³²The wicked watches the righteous,
   and seeks to slay him.
³³The LORD will not abandon him to his power,
   or let him be condemned when he is brought to trial.

³⁴Wait for the LORD, and keep to his way,
   and he will exalt you to possess the land;
   you will look on the destruction of the wicked.

³⁵I have seen a wicked man overbearing,
   and towering like a cedar of Lebanon.
³⁶Again I passed by, and, lo, he was no more;
   though I sought him, he could not be found.

³⁷Mark the blameless man, and behold the upright,
   for there is posterity for the man of peace.
³⁸But transgressors shall be altogether destroyed;
   the posterity of the wicked shall be cut off.

³⁹The salvation of the righteous is from the LORD;
   he is their refuge in the time of trouble.
⁴⁰The LORD helps them and delivers them;
   he delivers them from the wicked, and saves them,
   because they take refuge in him.

This psalm is also an acrostic, specifically alphabetical.
Unlike Psalms 34 and 112, Psalm 37 has two full lines for

each letter of the alphabet. Although it may first seem to be an accumulation of Israelite wisdom artificially strung on an alphabet, L. Alonso Schökel has plausibly suggested that the psalm deals with the problem of social justice. The author presents himself as an older sage (vv 25,35-36) who recognizes the problem of social justice faced by his younger audience (v7).[35]

The psalmist initiates his handling of the social justice by mentioning the wrongdoers who will not have the final word (vv 1-2). In advocating trust, the sage touches the problem for the first time, viz., trusting and doing good will lead to dwelling in the land and enjoying security (v 3). In verse 6 the sage assures his audience that God will bring forth their innocence as the light and their justice as the noonday. In verse 9 he distinguishes between the fate of the just and the unjust. While the wicked will be cut off, those waiting for Yahweh will possess the land. The land motif reappears in verse 11 where the meek are promised prosperity in addition to land possession. Verse 12 vividly portrays the plotting of the wicked against the righteous by noting the grinding of teeth. In verse 22 the blessed and the cursed are distinguished. The former shall possess the land while the latter shall be cut off. Finally in verse 29 the poet adds that the righteous will dwell in the land forever.

In view of such heinous violations of human justice the sage offers timely advice. He emphasizes that Yahweh is not immune to or oblivious of such violations. The God of Israel is a committed deity. According to verse 3 the proper reaction is trust in Yahweh. Furthermore, Yahweh will not abandon the righteous to the power of the unrighteous nor will he pronounce the righteous guilty at the time of trial (v 33). In the other direction the socially oppressed should not take matters into their own hands. They are to curb their anger since it will only lead to evil (v 8).

In verses 37-38 the author develops the notion of time

with regard to the righteous and the unrighteous. Instead of RSV "posterity" in these verses one may also translate "future." Since retribution occurs only on earth, the "future" of humans is exceedingly important. Perdue writes: " . . . the 'future' of a man . . . includes every element of one's hopes for his future: longevity, descendants, success, prosperity, well-being, etc."[36] According to the psalmist's theology only the righteous will have a "future" since the wicked will be utterly cut off.

At prayer we must not allow ourselves to be lulled into complacency by focusing merely on the needs of our minuscule world. Prayer is the locus for the shocks and atrocities noted in our newspapers and paraded on our television sets. Covenant will not permit us to tune out the cries of the socially oppressed. Where there is social oppression, there is disorder. And where there is disorder, there is a situation which the wise cannot tolerate. Prayer must move into the "future" of the psalmist so that pain will be redressed now and the land will be returned now. Prayer and social justice go hand in hand. To pray this psalm and then to neglect social justice is not to pray at all.

New Testament

Luke 6:20-21

[20]And he lifted up his eyes on his disciples, and said:

"Blessed are you poor, for yours is the kingdom of God.

[21]"Blessed are you that hunger now, for you shall be satisfied.

"Blessed are you that weep now, for you shall laugh."

According to J. Dupont[37] Jesus originally pronounced these beatitudes in the third person, e.g., "Blessed are the poor, for theirs is the kingdom of heaven." As such, they

---

[36]L. Perdue, *Wisdom and Cult*, 285.

[37]J. Dupont, *Les Béatitudes: Tome I, Le problème littéraire* (2d ed.; Paris: Gabalda, 1958) 272-298. See also W. Harrington, *The Gospel According to St. Luke. A Commentary* (New York: Newman, 1967) 100-111.

correspond to the formulation of the wisdom psalms. Against the background of the Old Testament Jesus presents himself as a wise man, as one bent upon offering a guide for steering through life. These beatitudes may be understood, therefore, as Jesus' plan for harmony, balance, and equilibrium in the Father's kingdom. They speak to that situation where existence will become celebration because all needs will be met. Jesus' ministry is the occasion for pronouncing the poor, the mourning, and the hungry blessed because this sage has set out to reverse their lot. It should be noted that Jesus' audience is not deemed blessed because of their spiritual qualities but because of God's action in Jesus. [38]

In the programmatic sermon in the Nazareth synagogue (Luke 4:16-30) [39] Luke has Jesus outline his ministry in terms of Isaiah 58:6; 61:1-2: "'The Spirit of the Lord is upon me, because he has anointed me to preach good news to the poor. He has sent me to proclaim release to the captives and recovering of sight to the blind, to set at liberty those who are oppressed . . .'" (Luke 4:18). For Luke this sermon provides the substance of the preaching of Jesus. Against the background of the Beatitudes Jesus is once more the wise man who announces the end of disharmony and disillusion and the start of harmony and hope. ". . . , he makes us understand that his mission concerns the unfortunate; he must proclaim to them the end of their suffering." [40] What is significant is that Jesus understands the return of God's order as linked to his own person. In him the wisdom psalms take on a deeper reality.

In both Matthew and Luke Jesus dispels the doubts of the

---

[38] See J. Dupont, "The Poor and Poverty in the Gospels and Acts," *Gospel Poverty: Essays in Biblical Theology* (ed. M. D. Guinan; Chicago: Franciscan Herald Press, 1977) 39-40; M. D. Guinan, *Gospel Poverty: Witness to the Risen Christ*, 62-63.

[39] See J. Dupont, "The Salvation of the Gentiles and the Theological Significance of Acts," *The Salvation of the Gentiles: Essays on the Acts of the Apostles* (New York: Paulist, 1979) 11-33, esp. 20-22.

[40] J. Dupont, "The Poor and Poverty," 35.

Baptist concerning the Father's mission (see Matt 11:2-6; Luke 7:18-23).[41] It is not the fire and brimstone envisioned by the Baptist (see Matt 3:11-12; Luke 3:16-17). It is, rather, the healing of the blind, the cripples, the lepers, and the deaf as well as the raising of the dead and the preaching of the Good News to the poor. John was scandalized by Jesus' sense of mission. In correcting John's view Jesus utters a beatitude: "'And blessed is he who takes no offense at me'" (Matt 11:6; Luke 7:23). For Jesus, mission consists in overcoming all those obstacles which make living less than celebration. In Jesus' world a fully human life is a gift to be cherished in community, not a down payment to be honored in the celestial banking house.

In the Book of Proverbs wisdom is personified as God's unique creature.[42] She beckons to humans to accept God's view of reality and act accordingly. "Does not wisdom call, does not understanding raise her voice? On the heights beside the way, in the paths she takes her stand . . ." (Prov 8:1-2).[43] In chapter 9 Lady Wisdom, having built her house, invites the wise to partake of her table: "'Come, eat of my bread and drink of the wine I have mixed'" (Prov 9:5). In Eucharist the exhortations and the teachings of God's Sage par excellence are set against the background of bread and wine. To partake of the bread and the cup is to share the world view of this Sage.[44] To be welcomed to this table means to translate that wisdom into action whereby our distorted world becomes less chaotic and disorganized. To

[41] See J. Dupont, "L'ambassade de Jean-Baptiste (Matthieu 11,2-6; Luc 7,18-23)," *Nouvelle revue théologique* 83 (1961) 805-821, 943-959; J. F. Craghan," "A Redactional Study of Lk 7,21 in the Light of Dt 19,15," *CBQ* 29 (1967) 47-61 = 353-367.

[42] See B. Lang, *Frau Weisheit: Deutung einer biblischen Gestalt* (Düsseldorf: Patmos, 1975).

[43] Proverbs 1-9 is inspired by both the Torah and the prophets. For this view see R. Tournay, "Proverbs 1-9: A First Theological Synthesis of the Tradition of the Sages," *The Dynamism of Biblical Tradition* (ed. P. Benoit et al.; Concilium 20; New York: Paulist, 1967) 51-61.

[44] For Eucharist as normative "Eucharistia" see H. H. Guthrie, *Theology as Thanksgiving*, 188-195.

recite the Eucharistic prayer is to imbibe a wisdom whereby the participants become bread and wine for others. Eucharist becomes "the good life" only insofar as other humans are made whole and thus rendered capable of celebrating, not just tolerating life.

Summary of the theology of the wisdom psalms[45]

(1) Harmony, order, and balance are to be reflected not only in the universe but also in the lives of fellow humans.

(2) Wisdom of the plan for achieving this equilibrium is rooted in a person, Yahweh, and in respect for and openness to Yahweh's plan, i.e., "fear of the Lord."

(3) Genuine human life is one in which celebration is paramount. Life is not merely a passage or a condition for making it in the hereafter. Life is a gift from the Creator to be shared in community.

(4) True wisdom is not an ego trip. To have a good life also means to better the lives of others. To be happy is to make others happy. "...the wise have discerned that *we* precedes *me* theologically, chronologically, and logically."[46]

(5) Although the formulation "righteousness = success, wickedness = failure" is faulted by our own experience, wisdom recommends that we seek to extol goodness and denounce evil in this life.

---

[45] Other wisdom psalms include the following: 32, 49. Wisdom elements are found in the following psalms: 25:8-10,12-14; 31:23-24; 39:4-6; 40:4-5; 62:8-10; 92:6-8; 94:8-15.

[46] W. Brueggemann, "Scripture and an Ecumenical Life-Style," 10 (author's italics).

5

Prayers for the Institution
The Royal Psalms

Personal versus communal good

Ideally at least political offices envision the common good, not personal aggrandizement. However, frequently the politician is not the one who realizes the expectations of the community. Somehow we have come to accept as a fact of life that new titles and new offices mean the enhancement of the holder, not the improvement of the people. Nonetheless to be a leader means to exist for others. As a result, the community has a right to expect a reasonable degree of performance.

The temptation to exploit power is not limited to high government officials. We observe it in our own families and local communities. The bearer of a title, e.g., husband/wife, father/mother, employer/employee, may manipulate another or others out of purely selfish interests. Perhaps one of our greatest challenges is the mature use of the power conferred on us by our family position, job, or society at large. Indeed no one is exempt from the egotistical drive of power, not even our church and its officials. Comparing Matthew 5:29-30 (the prohibition against lust) and 18:6-14 (scandal or care of the little ones), J. P. Meier writes: "Mt used a similar exhortation to spiritual rather than physical integrity in 5:29-30. There it forbade sexual lust in the individual; here it forbids lust for power in the church.

Ambition is the cleric's lust."[1]

In the theology of the ancient Near East the king held a sacral position between the gods and the people. S. Mowinckel describes this position in the following way:

> "The king is thus the representative of the gods on earth, the steward of the god or gods. Through him they exercise their power and sovereignty, and he is the channel through which blessing and happiness and fertility flow from the gods to men.

> "But he is also man's representative before the gods. In him the people is one. According to the corporate view of those times the people was somehow incorporated in him, and the strength and blessing which he receives from the gods were partaken of by the whole country and the people."[2]

As the traditions in First Samuel 7-15 show,[3] kingship did not emerge easily in Israel. Political realities such as the Philistine oppression made it a necessity. While Israel, however, could not accept the pagan implications of the royal ideology of the ancient Near East, she did understand the king as the mediator between Yahweh and the people.

---

[1] J. P. Meier, *Matthew*, 203. See also 293.

[2] S. Mowinckel, *The Psalms in Israel's Worship*, I. 51. For the significance of the king in the psalms, see H. –J. Kraus, *Theologie der Psalmen*, 134-155.

[3] See H. J. Boecker, *Die Beurteilung der Anfänge des Königtums in den deuteronomistischen Abschnitten des I. Samuelbuches* (Wissenschaftliche Monographien zum Alten und Neuen Testament 31; Neukirchen-Vluyn: Neukirchener Verlag, 1969); J. A. Soggin, *Das Königtum in Israel: Ursprünge, Spannungen, Entwicklung* (Beihefte zur Zeitschrift für die alttestamentliche Wissenschaft 104; Berlin: Töpelmann, 1967) 27-76; F. M. Cross, *Canaanite Myth and Hebrew Epic*, 220-273; B. C. Birch, *The Rise of the Israelite Monarchy: The Growth and Development of 1 Samuel 7-15* (Society of Biblical Literature Dissertation Series 27; Missoula, Montana: Scholars Press, 1976); A. D. H. Mayes, "The Period of the Judges and the Rise of the Monarchy," *Israelite and Judaean History* (ed. J. H. Hayes & J. M. Miller; Old Testament Library; Philadelphia: Westminster, 1977) 285-331; B. Halpern, *The Constitution of the Monarchy in Israel* (Harvard Semitic Monographs 25; Chico, California: Scholars Press, 1981).

Ideally "Long live the king!" meant "Long live the people!"[4]

At prayer we cannot avoid the implications of our own royalty. According to the opening chapters of Genesis God freely chooses to run the risk of monarchy. He makes men and women kings and queens so that they may be the instruments of his concern for others. Hence in praying these psalms, we are also addressed.[5] We are invited not only to sense the headiness of our royal prerogatives but also to test the reality of our royal accomplishments.[6] At prayer we are asked whether we have made our contribution to the harmony, peace, and equilibrium of our royal domain. Thus prayer is that dangerous rendezvous for reflecting on the reality of our obligations, not our rights. The royal psalms remind us and remind us forcefully that to have power means to empower others to a genuinely human life.

Royal psalms[7]

The royal psalms are prayers related to the Davidic dynasty in Jerusalem. They are distinguished more by content

---

[4] Views about the Israelite adaptation of monarchy in the ancient Near East are at times quite desperate. G. E. Mendenhall ("The Monarchy," *Int* 29 [1975] 160) holds "that by the end of Solomon's regime the Jerusalem state was a thoroughly paganized Syro-Hittite regime and was condemned as intolerable by the prophets, who represented the continuity of the Yahwist tradition." On the other hand, S. Talmon ("Kingship and the Ideology of the State," *The Age of the Monarchies: Culture and Society* [ed. A. Malamat; The Word History of the Jewish People, 5; Jerusalem: Massada, 1979] 4-7) maintains that because of religious and doctrinal values monarchy in Israel was necessarily different from that of the ancient Near East.

[5] It is useful to note that by the time of Second Isaiah (see Isa 55:1-5) there was a certain deomocratization of the oracle to David. See O. Eissfeldt, "The Promises of Grace to David in Isaiah 55:1-5," *Israel's Prophetic Heritage: Essays in Honor of James Muilenburg,* 196-207, esp. 202-207; W. Brueggemann, "Isaiah 55 and Deuteronomic Theology," *ZAW* 80 (1968) 191-203.

[6] For the dignity and prerogative of monarchy as the possession of every Israelite see J. A. Fischer, "Everyone a King: A Study of the Psalms," *The Bible Today* 97 (Oct., 1978) 1683-1689.

[7] For a study of the royal psalms in the setting of an annual royal ritual in which the king was subjected to humiliation and exaltation see A. R. Johnson, *Sacral*

than by literary characteristics. Hence they have no special literary structure. For example, Psalms 2, 21, 72, 101, and 110 celebrate the king's coronation or its anniversary. Psalm 45 is a poem for a royal wedding. Psalm 18 is a thanksgiving for the king's victory while Psalm 20 is a prayer for the king's victory. It is significant that these psalms do not refer to a specific king. Rather, they celebrate the type of the true king. In this sense one may speak of them as prayers for the institution.

According to the theology of these psalms the king is Yahweh's "messiah." As Yahweh's anointed one (the meaning of "messiah"), he is the human instrument of God's concern for the people. In keeping with the royal ideology of the ancient Near East he is the incorporation of his people. He is also Yahweh's adopted son. Every Davidic king has the right to lay claim to Nathan's oracle: " '"I will be his father (the reference is to David's line), and he shall be my son. When he commits iniquity, I will chasten him with the rods of men; but I will not take my steadfast love from him . . . And your house and your kingdom shall be made sure for ever before me; your throne shall be established for ever" ' " (2 Sam 7:14-16).[8] It is remarkable that Israel continued to pray these psalms after the sixth century B. C. when there

---

Kingship in Ancient Israel (2d ed.; Cardiff: University of Wales, 1967). For an application of A. R. Johnson's ideas see K. Crim, *Royal Psalms* (Richmond: John Knox, 1962).

[8] On the significance of this oracle, its theological implications, and its tension with the Sinai covenant see the following studies: "L. Rost, "Sinaibund und Davidsbund," *Theologische Literaturzeitung* 72 (1947) 129-134; J. L. McKenzie, "The Dynastic Oracle," *TS* 8 (1947) 187-218; R. E. Clements, *Prophecy and Covenant* (Studies in Biblical Theology 43; Naperville, Illinois: Allenson, 1965) 56-68; D. J. McCarthy, "II Samuel 7 and the Structure of the Deuteronomic History," *JBL* 84 (1965) 131-138; P. Calderone, *Dynastic Oracle and Suzerainty Treaty* (Logos 1; Manila: Loyola House of Studies, 1966); M. Weinfeld, "The Covenant of Grant in the Old Testament and the Ancient Near East," *Journal of the American Oriental Society* 90 (1970) 184-203; R. de Vaux, "The King of Israel, Vassal of Yahweh," *The Bible and the Ancient Near East* (Garden City, New York: Doubleday, 1971) 152-166; K. Seybold, *Das davidische Königtum im Zeugnis der*

was no remaining Davidic monarch.[9] By continuing to pray these psalms and by making psalm 2 the introduction to the Psalter (along with Psalm 1), Israel entertained the hope that eventually there would be another royal presence in her midst.[10]

Psalm 132[11]

Remember, O Lord, in David's favor,
all the hardships he endured;
[2]how he swore to the LORD
and vowed to the Mighty One of Jacob,
[3]"I will not enter my house
or get into my bed;
[4]I will not give sleep to my eyes
or slumber to my eyelids,
[5]until I find a place for the LORD,
a dwelling place for the Mighty One of Jacob."

[6]Lo, we heard of it in Eph'rathah,
we found it in the field of Ja'ar.
[7]"Let us go to his dwelling place;

Propheten (Forschungen zur Religion und Literatur des Alten und Neuen Testaments 107; Göttingen: Vandenhoeck & Ruprecht, 1972); F. M. Cross, *Canaanite Myth and Hebrew Epic*, 241-264; J. Bright, *Covenant and Promise: The Prophetic Understanding of the Future in Pre-Exilic Israel* (Philadelphia: Westminster, 1976); J. D. Levenson, "The Davidic Covenant and Its Modern Interpreters," *CBQ* 41 (1979) 205-219.

[9] F. M. Cross (*Canaanite Myth and Hebrew Epic*, 274-289) holds that there were two editions of the Deuteronomistic History: (a) one written in the era of Josiah as a programmatic document of his reform and of his revival of the Davidic state; (b) another composed around 550 B. C. to update the history and change the work into a sermon on history addressed to the Judean exiles. This twofold edition would help to explain why the promise to David is absolute in 2 Samuel 7:14-16 but conditional in such texts as 1 Kings 2:4; 8:25; 9:4-5. On this twofold edition see now R. D. Nelson, *The Double Redaction of the Deuteronomistic History (JSOT* Supplement Series 18; Sheffield: University of Sheffield, 1981).

[10] See B. S. Childs, *Introduction to the Old Testament as Scripture.* 515-517.

[11] See A. Weiser, *The Psalms*, 778-782; H. -J. Kraus, *Psalmen*, 876-888; H. H. Guthrie, *Israel's Sacred Songs*, 103-106.

let us worship at his footstool!"
⁸Arise, O LORD, and go to thy resting place,
  thou and the ark of thy might.
⁹Let thy priests be clothed with righteousness,
  and let thy saints shout for joy.
¹⁰For thy servant David's sake
  do not turn away the face of thy anointed one.

¹¹The LORD swore to David a sure oath
  from which he will not turn back:
"One of the sons of your body
  I will set on your throne.
¹²If your sons keep my covenant
  and my testimonies which I shall teach them,
  their sons also for ever
    shall sit upon your throne."
¹³For the LORD has chosen Zion;
  he has desired it for his habitation:
¹⁴"This is my resting place for ever;
  here I will dwell, for I have desired it.
¹⁵I will abundantly bless her provisions;
  I will satisfy her poor with bread.
¹⁶Her priests I will clothe with salvation,
  and her saints will shout for joy.
¹⁷There I will make a horn to sprout for David;
  I have prepared a lamp for my anointed.
¹⁸His enemies I will clothe with shame,
  but upon himself his crown will shed its luster."

This royal psalm is a liturgy commemorating Yahweh's covenant with David and his choice of Zion.¹² However, it is not clear on which precise feast this liturgy was celebrated. It may be divided as follows: (a) a prayer for David because

¹²Zion first referred to the Jebusite city that David conquered — hence the name "city of David" (see 2 Sam 5:7). Later it signified the larger metropolis of Jerusalem (see Isa 10:24). Still later it designated that part of the city on the northeast which was occupied by the temple (Ps 132:13).

of his great concern for Yahweh's dwelling place (vv 1-5) —
this prayer was probably read by a priest or some cultic
official; (b) the ritual of the processional bearing of the ark
into Jerusalem (vv 6-10) in which the choir would recite the
story of David's discovery of the ark; (c) Yahweh's promise
of an eternal (though conditional) dynasty (vv 11-12); (d)
Yahweh's everlasting choice of Zion (vv 13-18).

In the first section the psalmist exaggerates David's
preoccupation with the ark, i.e., the footstool of God's
throne,[13] by creating an oath whereby David will not sleep
until the ark is found. Unlike the story in Second Samuel
6:1-15, Psalm 132 presupposes that the location of the ark is
not known (v 6).[14] When, however, it is discovered, the choir
takes up the old battle cry (see Num 10:35-36) that Yahweh
now move from his present dwelling place to his new one in
Jerusalem (v 8). This transfer becomes the occasion for
appealing for victory on behalf of the priests and faithful (v
9) and the Davidic king (v 10). In the third section the
psalmist speaks of Yahweh's oath (v 11) to David (no longer
a promise as in Second Samuel 7). According to F. M. Cross
the conditional covenant here (v 12: "'. . . *If* your sons keep my
covenant . . .'") reflects the early reign of David with its
greater insistence on obedience.[15] Hence David is not an
absolute monarch — he is answerable to his God and in turn
is answerable to the needs of the people. In the final section
Yahweh's taking possession of his new resting place means

[13] See R. de Vaux, *Ancient Israel*, 294-302; "Ark of the Covenant and Tent of
Reunion," *The Bible and the Ancient Near East*, 136-151.

[14] See F. M. Cross, *Canaanite Myth and Hebrew Epic*, 97. For the different
levels in Second Samuel 6 see A. F. Campbell, *The Ark Narrative (1 Sam 4-6; 2
Sam 6): A Form-Critical and Traditio-Historical Study* (Society of Biblical Literature Dissertation Series 16; Missoula, Montana: Scholars Press, 1975) 101-117.

[15] F. M. Cross, *Canaanite Myth and Hebrew Epic*, 233. T. E. Fretheim ("Psalm
132: A Form Critical Study," *JBL* 86 [1967] 289-300) also observes that the
relationship of verses 1-5 and 10-12 is the same as the relationship between Second
Samuel 6 and 7. C. B. Houk ("Psalm 132, Literary Integrity and Syllable-Word
Structures," *JSOT 6* [1978] 41-48) agrees with Cross and Fretheim that verses 1-5,
11-12 are different from verses 6-10. He also maintains that verses 13-14 reflect a
theology different from verses 11-12.

the fulfillment of the petitions in verses 9-10. After mentioning Yahweh's provision for the poor, the priests, and the devout (vv 15-16), the author directs most of his attention to David. Thus David will have descendants (v 17: "'a horn to sprout for David'"), he will experience security and divine presence (v 17: "'a lamp for my anointed'"), and he will see the downfall of his enemies and the glory of his own reign (v 18).

At prayer we cannot help but be overwhelmed by the interaction of human effort and divine grace in this psalm. To David's oath to find the ark there corresponds Yahweh's oath to create the Davidic dynasty. There is here a dimension of intimacy which we must relish but an intimacy which is linked to obedience to the God of the covenant. In anticipating the honors and grandeur of royalty, we must also bear in mind the condition attached to them, viz., Yahweh's covenant and testimonies (v 12). To be treated as kings and queens means that we have upheld and promoted the royal character of our fellow humans. It is only intimacy translated into obedience that creates the kingdom where order, stability, and equilibrium reign. At prayer we are reminded that the only fitting royal emblem is service to others.

Psalm 2[16]

> Why do the nation's conspire,
> and the peoples plot in vain?
> [2]The kings of the earth set themselves,
>   and the rulers take counsel together,
>   against the LORD and his anointed, saying,
> [3]"Let us burst their bonds asunder,
>   and cast their cords from us."
>
> [4]He who sits in the heavens laughs;

---

[16]See S. Mowinckel, *He That Cometh* (Oxford: Blackwell, 1956) 62-69; A. Weiser, *The Psalms*, 108-116; G. H. Jones, "'The Decree of Yahweh.' Ps. II,7" *VT* 15 (1965) 336-344; H. -J. Kraus, *Psalmen*, 11-22; S. Terrien, *The Elusive Presence*, 293-295.

the LORD has them in derision.

⁵Then he will speak to them in his wrath,
   and terrify them in his fury, saying,
⁶"I have set my king
   on Zion, my holy hill."

⁷I will tell of the decree of the LORD:
   He said to me, "You are my son,
      today I have begotten you.
⁸Ask of me, and I will make the nations your heritage,
   and the ends of the earth your possession.
⁹You shall break them with a rod of iron,
   and dash them in pieces like a potter's vessel."

¹⁰Now therefore, O kings, be wise;
   be warned, O rulers of the earth.
¹¹Serve the LORD with fear,
   with trembling ¹²kiss his feet,
   lest he be angry, and you perish in the way;
   for his wrath is quickly kindled.
   Blessed are all who take refuge in him.

This psalm is an early composition of pre-Israelite origin which was adapted to celebrate the accession or the anniversary of the accession of the Davidic king to the throne in Jerusalem. It presupposes the ritual of coronation which can be pieced together from other biblical texts.[17] It may be divided as follows: (a) description of the vassal nations in revolt (vv 1-3); (b) Yahweh's response to this situation (vv 4-6); (c) Yahweh's oracle announcing the king's legitimacy and firm rule (vv 7-9); (d) Yahweh's admonition to the vassal kings (and indirectly to the Davidic king) to obey the divine will.[18]

   In the first section the psalmist describes the dangers of

[17] See R. de Vaux, *Ancient Israel*, 100-114.

[18] P. Auffret (*The Literary Structure of Psalm 2 JSOT* Supplementary Series 3; Sheffield: University of Sheffield, 1977) concludes that the text of psalm 2 provides

interregnum. In the transition from one Davidic king to another vassal nations invariably seize the opportunity to rebel and thus throw off the Davidic yoke. In the absence of a king balance and harmony are jeopardized. It is likely that a temple choir sings of this international plot in verses 1-2 while a special choir quotes their intent in verse 3: "'Let us burst their bonds asunder, and cast their cords from us.'" In the second section Yahweh's reaction echoes from heaven to earth. In verses 4-5 the temple choir proclaims that reaction whereby laughter gives way to anger. The message is that Yahweh is very much in control. In verse 6 Yahweh speaks through a prophet or court official who anoints the crown prince. In the third section a prophet or court official speaks on behalf of Yahweh, citing the written document of legitimation, thereby authenticating the king. He is nothing less than God's son (v 7). Because of that status the new Davidic king is empowered by Yahweh to exercise firm world dominion and thus restore the world to harmony and balance (vv 8-9). In the final section the vassal kings are urged to comply and do obeisance whereby laughter gives way to anger. The message is to the new king since Yahweh rules the world through him.

For the people gathered at the ceremony this psalm evoked the attitude of "Happy days are here again!" It was indeed an atmosphere of orientation since God's pledged word guaranteed peace, security, and hope. Although the threat of vassal nations was a reality for only a limited period of time and hence is a borrowing from the court style of the ancient Near East, it did serve to underline Yahweh's commitment to the Davidic king and through him to the people. Thus, while the psalm is a prayer for the institution,

two types of symmetry: (a) parallel symmetry (vv 1-3 = vv 7-9) and vv 4-6 = vv 10-12); and (b) concentric symmetry (vv 1-3 = vv 10-12 and vv 4-6 = vv 7-9). He concludes (p. 31): "We have here then a process that is typical of our author, which allows him at one and the same time to set Yahweh and his king at the heart of his poem (vv. 4-9) and to put in parallel two short narratives in which the initiative belongs in the one case to the nations (vv. 1-6) and in the other to Yahweh (vv. 7-12)."

it is also a prayer for those protected by the institution. Exuberance, therefore, could be the only natural reaction to such good news.

Israel never regarded the king as a god. However, in the development of the royal ideology with Solomon and his temple the distance between the king and the people widened. This royal psalm implied more than "Hail to the Chief." It made the head of state the object of flattery and adulation. As S. Terrien has observed, "A coronation hymn which included the oracle 'Today, I have begotten thee' tended to separate the anointed monarch from other human beings not only socially but also ontologically. The notion of sacred sonship, even viewed as the result of ritual adoption, tended to blur the sharp distinction which Mosaic Yahwism had maintained between the human and divine realms."[19]

At prayer we are confronted by the disharmony and disorder in our world and our own royal ego. Our temptation is to interpret our royal status as a condition which admits us to the world of the divine and thereby excludes us and indeed exempts us from the world of the profane. We note that we find it consoling to isolate ourselves in that world and neglect our royal charges. We are anesthesized into thinking that our coronation means a goal already achieved, not a goal to be achieved. We dare not think that the One who sits in heaven will laugh at us (v 4). Yet we must conclude that such thinking and acting are a distortion of our regal condition. Only a royalty that unshackles itself from heaven (see verse 3) and immerses itself in things of earth is genuine royalty. It is only when we create harmony and order among our subjects that we have truly earned the title of king or queen. Ultimately the temptation faced by the Davidic king to blur the distinction between the sacred and the profane is healthy and very much alive in our midst.

[19] S. Terrien, *The Elusive Presence*, 294.

Psalm 45[20]

My heart overflows with a goodly theme,
I address my verses to the king;
My tongue is like the pen of a ready scribe.

[2]You are the fairest of the sons of men;
grace is poured upon your lips;
therefore God has blessed you for ever.
[3]Gird your sword upon your thigh, O mighty one,
in your glory and majesty!

[4]In your majesty ride forth victoriously
for the cause of truth and to defend the right;
let your right hand teach you dread deeds!
[5]Your arrows are sharp in the heart of the king's enemies;
the people fall under you.

[6]Your divine throne endures for ever and ever.
Your royal scepter is a scepter of equity;
[7]   you love righteousness and hate wickedness.
Therefore God, your God, has anointed you
with the oil of gladness above your fellows;
[8]   your robes are all fragrant with myrrh and aloes and
cassia.
From ivory palaces stringed instruments make you glad;
[9]   daughters of kings are among your ladies of honor;
at your right hand stands the queen in gold of Ophir.
[10]Hear, O daughter, consider, and incline your ear;
forget your people and your father's house;
[11]   and the king will desire your beauty.
Since he is your lord, bow to him;
[12]   the people of Tyre will sue your favor with gifts,
the richest of the people [13]with all kinds of wealth.
The princess is decked in her chamber with gold-woven
robes;

---

[20]See A. Weiser, *The Psalms*, 360-365; H. –J. Kraus, *Psalmen*, 330-338; P. J.
King, *A Study of Psalm 45 (44)* (Rome: Lateran University, 1959).

¹⁴   in many-colored robes she is led to the king,
     with her virgin companions, her escort, in her train.
¹⁵With joy and gladness they are led along
     as they enter the palace of the king.

¹⁶Instead of your fathers shall be your sons;
     you will make them princes in all the earth.
¹⁷I will cause your name to be celebrated in all generations;
     therefore the peoples will praise you for ever and ever.

This royal psalm is the celebration of a royal wedding. Although its original setting was perhaps the marriage of a northern king to a foreign princess (see Tyre in verse 12), it was eventually adapted to the southern kingdom and its Davidic dynasty. (This may explain why the king may be addressed as *'elōhîm* or "god" in verse 6, i.e., a sacral person beyond the ordinary — see Isa 7:14). The psalm may be divided as follows: (a) introduction by the court poet (v 1); (b) the poet's praise of the king (vv 2-9); (c) address by the queen mother²¹ to the princess chosen (vv 10-12); (d) a description of the bride's apparel and the procession (vv 13-15); (e) the poet's concluding address to the king (vv 16-17).

In L. Alonso Schökel's analysis an eloquent and handsome king, who is a victor in battle and a just ruler, is going to celebrate a marriage. There are various pretenders of royal blood and he has fallen in love with one of them. His mother, i. e., the queen mother mentioned in verse 9,²³ assists him in the ceremony by soliciting the consent of the chosen (vv 10-11). The other pretenders now withdraw and the lucky princess is led to the king (v 14a) while her entour-

²¹ For the identification of the queen in verse 9 as the queen mother see L. Alonso Schökel, *Treinta Salmos*, 173-176.

²² *Ibid.*, 176-179.

²³ On the political position of the queen mother or Great Lady see R. de Vaux, *Ancient Israel*, 117-119. According to First Kings 15:13 the queen mother or Great Lady is actually the grandmother of the king.

age is led to the palace (v 15). Finally the poet wishes the king sons upon whom he will confer offices. The personages in the poem are, therefore, the following: the king, the queen mother, the various royal princesses (would-be wives of the king), and the princess selected by the king along with her entourage. However, the central figure is clearly the king. The court poet sings his praises in verses 2-9, the queen mother observes in verse 12 that the king finds the lucky princess irresistible, and in verse 16 the poet implies that the successor to the throne will be the son of this fortunate woman.

While the climate of the psalm is clearly festive because of the marriage of the handsome king and the beautiful princess, the psalmist also emphasizes other values.[24] According to verse 4 the king champions truth and justice. According to verse 7 he advocates the right order of society, viz., the promotion of righteousness[25] and the overthrow of wickedness. Thus the king adds to his beauty a profound sense of covenant loyalty and fidelity. The lucky lady is getting a first-class husband.

At prayer we reflect on the exuberance of marriage celebrations but more particularly on the sense of loyalty and fidelity demanded by such celebrations. As kings and queens, human spouses are to create an atmosphere of stability and equilibrium in their relationships. As this psalm suggests, qualities such as truth, justice, and righteousness are those factors which contribute to this atmosphere. At prayer we cannot exclude the analogy of royal marriages in the relationship of a bishop to his diocese, especially of the Bishop of Rome. Here too the covenant qualities mentioned in this psalm come to the fore. True

---

[24] On the scepter in verse 6 as the symbol of divine blessings on the king because of his covenant fidelity see J. P. J. Olivier, "The Sceptre of Justice and Ps 45:7b," *Journal of Northwest Semitic Languages* 7 (1979) 45-54.

[25] On the notion of righteousness in the royal psalms see A. R. Johnson, *Sacral Kingship in Ancient Israel*, 3-9, 35-37.

harmony means that the people are served, not the bishop, that the common good is fostered, not personal ambition, that the obligations of the bishop are stressed, not his rights. At the same time we must honestly ask ourselves how we have assisted the bishop and other church leaders in promoting the well-being of our local diocese or church. Royalty makes such demands. At prayer we dare not avoid all the implications of such marriages.

Psalm 72[26]

> Give the king thy justice, O God,
>   and thy righteousness to the royal son!
> [2]May he judge thy people with righteousness,
>   and thy poor with justice!
> [3]Let the mountains bear prosperity for the people,
>   and the hills, in righteousness!
> [4]May he defend the cause of the poor of the people,
>   give deliverance to the needy, and crush the oppressor!
>
> [5]May he live while the sun endures,
>   and as long as the moon, throughout all generations!
>
> [6]May he be like rain that falls on the mown grass,
>   like showers that water the earth!
> [7]In his days may righteousness flourish,
>   and peace abound, till the moon be no more!
> [8]May he have dominion from sea to sea,
>   and from the River to the ends of the earth!
> [9]May his foes bow down before him,
>   and his enemies lick the dust!
> [10]May the kings of Tarshish and of the isles
>   render him tribute,

[26]See A. Weiser, *The Psalms,* 500-505; H.-J. Kraus, *Psalmen* 493-500; R. E. Murphy, *A Study of Psalm 72 (71)* (Washington, D.C.: Catholic University of America, 1948); P. W. Skehan, "Strophic Structure in Psalm 72," *Biblica* 40 (1959) 168-174. Skehan's article is reprinted in: *Studies in Israelite Poetry and Wisdom* (Catholic Biblical Quarterly Monograph Series 1; Washington, D.C.: The Catholic Biblical Association of America, 1971) 53-58.

may the kings of Sheba and Seba bring gifts!
[11]May all kings fall down before him,
   all nations serve him!

[12]For he delivers the needy when he calls,
   the poor and him who has no helper.
[13]He has pity on the weak and the needy,
   and saves the lives of the needy.
[14]From oppression and violence he redeems their life;
   and precious is their blood in his sight.

[15]Long may he live,
   may gold of Sheba be given to him!
May prayer be made for him continually,
   and blessings invoked for him all the day!
[16]May there be abundance of grain in the land;
   on the tops of the mountains may it wave;
   may its fruit be like Lebanon;
   and may men blossom forth from the cities
   like the grass of the field!
[17]May his name endure for ever,
   his fame continue as long as the sun!
May men bless themselves by him,
   all nations call him blessed!
[18]Blessed be the LORD, the God of Israel,
   who alone does wondrous things.
[19]Blessed be his glorious name for ever;
   may his glory fill the whole earth!
   Amen and Amen!
[20]The prayers of David, the son of Jesse, are ended.

This psalm was recited on the occasion of the king's coronation or its anniversary. Borrowing from the court style of the ancient Near East, it stresses the following motifs: justice, peace, long life, worldwide rule. The basis of the messianic hope is, of course, Yahweh's promise to the Davidic dynasty. The psalm may be divided as follows: (a) introduction summarizing Yahweh's promise (vv 1-3); (b) a series of strophes praising the king and anticipating his fulfillment of his royal duties (vv 4-7, 8-11, 12-14, 15); (c) conclusion emphasizing fertility and justice which looks back to the introduction (vv 16-17). (Verses 18-20 form the conclusion of Books One and Two of the Psalter.)

In the introduction the psalmist interprets the meaning of justice and righteousness.[27] These royal qualities whereby right order and truth prevail are meant to redound to the good of the people. Hence in verse 2 the poet observes that the people and the poor in particular are to be the beneficiaries of these qualities. In verse 3 the blessings of fertility are invoked for the people. The word "prosperity" translates the Hebrew *šālôm* or "peace." C. Stuhlmueller captures its nuances:

> "Most of all, Ps 72 represents the biblical sense of *shalom* or peace, the fullest integration of life's blessings, be these physical, emotional or religious, reaching into economics and politics, throughout the Israelite kingdom and across the world —the fullest union of heaven and earth, God and the human family."[28]

In the central section the psalmist prays that the king bestow fertility on the people (v 6: "like rain..., like showers"), the consequence of which is the harvest of righteousness and peace (v 7). In verses 8-11 the psalmist focuses on the power and expansion of the Davidic dynasty. In the florid court language that kingdom is to extend from the

---

[27] On justice as restoring the right order of things see S. Mowinckel, *The Psalms in Israel's Worship*, 1. 146-150. With regard to the king's judicial authority see K. W. Whitelam, *The Just King: Monarchical Judicial Authority in Ancient Israel (JSOT* Supplementary Series 12; Sheffield: University of Sheffield, 1979).

[28] C. Stuhlmueller, *Psalms*, 1. 320. See also G. Picht & H. E. Tödt (eds.), *Studien zur Friedensforschung I* (Stuttgart: Klett, 1969); W. Bruggemann, *Living Toward a Vision: Biblical Reflections on Shalom* (Philadelphia: United Church Press, 1976). For an abundant bibliography on the topic of peace see N. Lohfink (ed.), *Gewalt und Gewaltlosigkeit in Alten Testament*, 238-204. On the Priestly Writer's notion of stability as based on cult see N. Lohfink, "Biblical Witness to the Ideal of a Stable World," *Great Themes from the Old Testament*, 183-201.

borders of Egypt to the Euphrates River and from Transjordan to the islands of the Mediterranean Sea (v 8). Tribute (v 10) is to be forthcoming from the far west (Tarshish and the isles) and from the south (Sheba and Seba) while due homage comes from the rulers of the world, whether friend (v 11) or foe (v 9). However, in the midst of such power the psalmist does not neglect the prime objects of royal concern: the needy, the poor, the one who has no helper, the weak (vv 12-13). The combination of "blood" and "redeem" in verse 14 suggests that the king is bound to act on behalf of the disenfranchised because of a certain kinship bond.[29] (Although kings historically tended to take good care only of kings, the prophets did not cease to insist on the demands of justice, especially on behalf of the poor.[30]) Finally in verse 17 the psalmist seems to allude to Genesis 12:3 where Abraham (through the Davidic kings) is to be a source of blessings to all the communities of the earth. Against the background of the Davidic dynasty the king's name and fame will endure (v 17) on the ground that the king has met the needs of his people. It is only this condition that will ensure fertility and well-being (v 16).

At prayer we must move beyond the record of the Davidic kings. By and large they were dismal failures — they provided for themselves, not the people. Nonetheless the focus of the psalm is the king as person for others, especially the disenfranchised. As J. Muilenburg aptly noted, the royal virtue which is stressed here is humility:

> "A king's prestige and honor (*kabod*) lie in his compassion and justice. He is humble, not only because he knows he is a man, but because he knows he can fulfill his obligations to his people only by dependence upon the

---

[29] On the notion of *gō'ēl* or "redeemer" see C. Stuhlmueller, *Creative Redemption in Deutero-Isaiah* (Analecta Biblica 43; Rome: Biblical Institute Press, 1970) 99-131; S. Lyonnet & L. Sabourin, *Sin, Redemption, and Sacrifice* (Analecta Biblica 48; Rome: Biblical Institute Press, 1970) 79-119.

[30] See J. Craghan, *Love and Thunder*, 111-119.

source of all justice and righteousness. That is what
Psalm 72 and other royal petitions are telling us. *In Israel,
the sign of royalty is humility.* The responsibilities of
power weigh so heavily upon the king that he must hasten
to the sanctuary for help in his weakness."[31]

At prayer, as we attempt to create harmony and prosperity for our royal charges, we must frankly admit that we
cannot attain the goal merely by our own efforts. Prayer is
not the application of a Stoic iron will that hopefully results
in accomplishments. Prayer is the awareness that to fulfill
our office we need to lean upon Another and thus gather
strength by noting our weaknesses. At prayer we come to
realize that we can be kings and queens for our vassals only
by becoming vassals of the King.

Psalm 101[32]

I will sing of loyalty and of justice;
to thee, O LORD, I will sing.
[2]I will give heed to the way that is blameless.
Oh when wilt thou come to me?

I will walk with integrity of heart
within my house;
[3]I will not set before my eyes
anything that is base.
I hate the work of those who fall away;
it shall not cleave to me.
[4]Perverseness of heart shall be far from me;
I will know nothing of evil.

[5]Him who slanders his neighbor secretly
I will destroy.
The man of haughty looks and arrogant heart
I will not endure.

---

[31] J. Muilenburg, *The Way of Israel: Biblical Faith and Ethics* (Harper
Torchbook; New York: Harper & Row, 1961) 124 (author's italics).

[32] See A. Weiser, *The Psalms*, 647-650; H. -J. Kraus, *Psalmen*, 688-692.

⁶I will look with favor on the faithful
　　in the land,
　　that they may dwell with me;
　　he who walks in the way that is blameless
　　　　shall minister to me.
⁷No man who practices deceit
　　shall dwell in my house;
　　no man who utters lies
　　　　shall continue in my presence.

⁸Morning by morning I will destroy
　　all the wicked in the land,
　　cutting off all the evildoers
　　　　from the city of the LORD.

H. A. Kenik has made a very plausible case for situating this psalm on the occasion of the enthronement of the Davidic king. "In a dialogic exchange with a cultic leader, the king would respond to questions that focused upon the conduct that was the criterion for the royal leader, and that was expected for a suitable relationship with his people."³³ The psalm is structured as follows: (a) hymnic introduction (v 1); (b) body: (i) programmatic statement about the fitting moral behavior of the king (vv 2-3a); (ii) manner in which the king will carry out this ideal conduct (verses 3b-5 are the negative formulation while verses 6-7 are the positive formulation); (c) conclusion sealing the king's promise (v 8). The theme of the psalm is the peace and order among God's people which is made possible by the practice of justice.

In the introduction (v 1) the poet sings of Yahweh's covenant loyalty to the king and his people and of the king's justice whereby he provides right order and peace. Verses 2-3a present the royal code of behavior: the blameless way, integrity of heart in the king's house, and shunning what is base in his presence. In the negative formulation of this conduct the poet first mentions the king's attitude towards

---

³³ H. A. Kenik, "Code of Conduct for a King: Psalm 101," *JBL* 95 (1976) 398.

evil (v 3b) and follows this up with a triple specification of the evil: removing perverseness of heart (v 4a), destroying slanderers (v 5a), and not enduring the arrogant (v 5b). In the positive formulation of royal conduct the psalmist develops the king's attitude towards the people. He will regard them with favor (v 6a). Moreover, he will expect certain character traits of them: the blameless way (v 6b), avoiding deceit so as to dwell in the king's house (v 7a), and eschewing lies so as to continue in the king's presence (v 7b). These character traits refer back to the code of royal behavior in verses 2-3a. As Kenik aptly remarks, "the king and the people alike are challenged to a kind of behavior that distinguishes those invited to the covenant relationship with Yahweh."[34] The conclusion alludes to the judicial role of the king in the administration of justice since this customarily took place in the morning (see 2 Sam 15:2-3; Jer 21:11-12).

The notion of harmony and well-being reflected in this psalm suggests the interaction of wisdom and royal theology.[35] The accent lies on the creation of a peaceful and wholesome community. Justice and politics are hardly odd bedfellows in establishing this climate.[36] What disrupts this climate is the disharmony effected by those who speak and act in such a way that the common good and total well-being are jeopardized. What is significant in avoiding such disruption is the mutual effort of the king and the people. While the king is commissioned to provide justice and good order (see Prov 2:12; 4:14,22; 6:12,14; 8:15-16), the people are also committed to covenant responsibility. To be in covenant means to provide for all, especially the weakest in the community.

At prayer we reflect on our oaths, promises, vows, etc.

[34] Ibid., 393.

[35] See J. E. Weir, "The Perfect Way, A Study of Wisdom Motifs in Ps 101," *Evangelical Quarterly* 53 (1981) 51-59.

[36] On wisdom in the early monarchy see the discussion in D. F. Morgan, *Wisdom in the Old Testament Traditions*, 45-62, 158-160.

Simply by being members of society, we have obligations towards others. By belonging to a faith community, we have our theological grounding for those obligations, viz., covenant. Perhaps we may recall the inaugurations of our presidents when we anticipate the administration's platform. Hopefully we will also recollect our own enthusiastic responses on such occasion. "Ask not what your country will do for you — ask what you can do for your country" captures part of our response at least. However, we must also include those somewhat less grandiose inaugurations, e. g., marriage vows, job commitments, family promises, etc. We have to examine our consciences and inquire whether or not we have been true to our royal code of conduct. At the same time we must ask whether or not we have supported and helped those who rule over us. Peace and harmony will emerge only at the cost of our own efforts.

New Testament

Mark 1:14; 8:27-33

14Now after John was arrested, Jesus came into Galilee, preaching the gospel of God, 15and saying, "The time is fulfilled, and the kingdom of God is at hand; repent, and believe in the gospel."

27And Jesus went on with his disciples, to the villages of Caesarea Philippi; and on the way he asked his disciples, "Who do men say that I am?" 28And they told him, "John the Baptist; and others say, Elijah; and others one of the prophets." 29 And he asked them, "But who do you say that I am?" Peter answered him, "You are the Christ."30 And he charged them to tell no one about him.

31 And he began to teach them that the Son of man must suffer many things, and be rejected by the elders and the chief priests and the scribes, and be killed, and after three days rise again. 32And he said this plainly. And Peter took him, and began to rebuke him. 33But turning

and seeing his disciples, he rebuked Peter, and said, "Get behind me, Satan! For you are not on the side of God, but of men."

In Mark 1:14 Jesus announces that God's kingdom has finally arrived. By using the term "kingdom,"[37] Jesus proclaims that God's plan of providing for all the people has now begun in his person. "Kingdom" referred to the ideal of leadership expressed in the royal psalms. It conjured up all those ideals whereby the king would rule over his state in such a way that justice and peace would be the hallmark of his reign. "Kingdom" connoted power but power channeled toward the common good, not personal aggrandizement. In particular, "kingdom" meant that the poor, the needy, the down and out would be conspicuous objects of the king's concern. Jesus' message, therefore, was nothing short of good news. God was taking a final and definitive hand in human history and Jesus was to be the catalyst of that unique event.

In carrying out his Father's plan for the kingdom, Jesus communicated a profound sense of basic human values. He preached that to find yourself you should lose yourself (see Mk 8:34-35), that to be first you must become a servant (see Mk 9:33-35), that to be great you must be small (see Mk 10:42-44). The radical message of the kingdom was that to exercise the office of leader meant to forget oneself in ongoing service to those being led. The royal theology of the ancient Near East and particularly of the Davidic dynasty took flesh, not only in the words of Jesus, but also in his actions and hence his way of life. The message of the kingdom was simply a code of conduct for all would-be kings and queens.

Jesus had misgivings about some of the popular notions of kingship, i.e., messiahship which focused primarily on

---

[37] On the significance of this topic in New Testament research see R. H. Hiers, "Kingdom of God," *IDBSup*, 516.

the power and prestige of the ruler. Recognizing the manipulative tendencies of power and prestige, he resolved to win the hearts of his hearers and not simply buy them off. At Caesarea Philippi Mark presents Jesus as acknowledging the title of messiah, i.e., Christ, when Peter offered his view. However, Mark goes on to show Jesus qualifying the position of messiah. Jesus would attain that position only as a result of his passion, death, and resurrection. This messiah is a suffering messiah. As Mark continues, this interpretation of royal power is something that Peter regards as totally contradictory. For Peter, therefore, power and suffering do not go hand in hand. However, Mark concludes the episode by having Jesus observe that Peter's position is a perversion of God's plan. To accept Peter's view is to align oneself with the self-seeking and dehumanizing party of Satan. In the final analysis Peter is receiving a lecture on the proper understanding of the royal psalms.[38]

In his speeches in Acts Luke uses the royal psalms to interpret Jesus' exaltation. In Acts 2:30 he cites Psalm 132:11, viz., that one of David's descendants would sit upon his throne. In Acts 2:34-35 he quotes Psalm 110:1, viz., that through the resurrection Jesus has been enthroned in his glory as Lord or Yahweh. In Acts 13:33 he uses Psalm 2:7, viz., that Jesus is properly called "son" on the day of the resurrection and hence shares with God universal kingship.[39] J. Dupont summarizes the use of the psalms and especially the royal psalms. "In the Psalms God reveals his secret purposes, and those purposes are realized in the suffering of Christ and his heavenly exaltation. In the Psalms Christ expresses, through the mouth of David, his

[38] On Mark's redactional work in 8:27-33 see R. E. Brown et al., *Peter in the New Testament* (New York: Paulist, 1973) 64-69; A. Stock, *Call to Discipleship: A Literary Study of Mark's Gospel* (Good News Studies 1; Wilmington Delaware, Michael Glazier, 1982) 129-139, esp. 133-135.

[39] See F. X. Durrwell, *The Resurrection: A Biblical Study* (New York: Sheed & Ward, 1960) 112-113.

own feelings and attitudes in carrying out the work of our redemption."[40]

Summary of the theology of the royal psalms[41]

(1)   These psalms must lead us to focus on both the institution and ourselves, especially in the context of virtues and vices.

(2) These psalms are calculated to address us as empowered people who must reach out to sustain and protect our royal charges.

(3) These psalms are to remind us of our need for humility so that we may draw strength from our God in exercising our office.

(4) These psalms also teach us not to abdicate the scene and give up on the proper discharge of our office. Offices are always for others — hence our God chooses to need us for others.

(5) The praying of the royal psalms long after the collapse of the Davidic dynasty teaches us that the sinful institution is always linked to the Sinless One.

---

[40] J. Dupont, "Messianic Interpretation of the Psalms in the Acts of the Apostles," *The Salvation of the Gentiles*, 127.

[41] Other royal psalms include the following: 18, 20-21, 110.

6

Out of the Pits
The Laments

Orientation versus disorientation

The psalms of descriptive praise, the psalms of trust or confidence, the wisdom psalms, and the royal psalms imply a world of logic and cohesiveness. They speak to the times when order and tranquility are in command, when logic and reason hold sway, when balance and equilibrium rule. But our human experience must candidly confess those times when chaos and disorder take over, when turbulence and panic assume control, when pain and frustration manage our lives. Our world is now in the process of falling or has already fallen apart. We suffer the death of a love one. We contract a serious illness. We become the object of slander or gossip. We find it increasingly more difficult to pay the rent or the mortgage. We are rejected by our former friends. How difficult it now becomes to pray: "The Lord is my shepherd, I shall not want" (Ps 23:1).

All too painfully our human vulnerability betrays itself. When tragedy strikes, we discover our pitiful weakness. We have to acknowledge that we are subject to interest rates, the caprices of human friendship, and the destructibility of the human body. Our world is collapsing and with typically human logic we seek to rebuild it the old-fashioned way. Indeed these efforts at reconstruction are the greatest source of disillusion. We invoke the tried and true remedies of the past but they do not work. We recite the doctrines of our church community but they are ineffective. We remember that the God who afflicts us is the God who loves us[1] but it is not enough. We cling to the ever new miracles of modern medicine but they do not do the job. Basically we do not want the securities of the past to disappear, we are unwilling to let go.

Loneliness is the specter that haunts us. We feel we are individuals cut off from the mainstream of life and condemned to a hell where the gnawing pain is isolation. Community no longer exists, the only reality is aloofness and disinterest on the part of others. It is now that we admit that distress and lack of communication go hand in hand. We angrily concede that the source of our frustration is the inability to communicate. Yet at the same time we begin to glimpse the reality of redemption, viz., pain which is not shared is pain which cannot be healed.[2]

At prayer we deal with the real experiences of life. In the presence of our God we put aside all pretense and make-believe. We know that our frustration is real and that a Stoic effort to forget it will only increase the frustration. In communing with our God we are exhorted to face the situation with all its agony.[3] We are challenged not to resort to never-never land where the pain is not real and the anguish not genuine. In honest dialogue with our God the fact is that

---

[1] On this theology in the Book of Job see H. L. Ginsberg, "Job the Patient and Job the Impatient," *Congress Volume — Rome* (VTSup 17; Leiden: Brill, 1969) 108-109.

[2] N. Lohfink ("On the Enemies of the Sick in the Ancient Near East and in the Psalms," *Great Themes from the Old Testament*, 166) notes: "We, too, often discover that we cannot talk a sick person out of his fears. In Israel they taught their sick to express such fears in prayer." On such prayer see K. Seybold, *Das Gebet des Kranken im Alten Testament. Untersuchungen zur Bestimmung und Zuordnung der Krankheits - und Heilungspsalmen* (Beiträge zur Wissenschaft vom Alten und Neuen Testament 99; Stuttgart: Kohlhammer, 1973).

[3] On the rawness of the language of lament see W. Brueggemann, "Psalms and the Life of Faith," 11-14; *Praying the Psalms*, 27-36.

the bottom is falling out of life. However, these less than beautiful moments are now the new raw material of prayer.[4]

Laments

In both the individual and communal laments[5] we have to do with a person. In these prayers there is One to whom both the individual and the community can and must turn in order to be healed. The laments show clearly that in disorientation our pain and agony must be person-oriented. Hence we talk *to* our God, we do not talk *about* him. The laments do not simply register the givens about our distressful situation. They are not a computer readout enumerating all our ills. The prayer of lament is not a gripe session.[6] Yahweh is a person, not a machine. Yahweh is a listener, not an anonymous programmer. Yahweh is our intimate, not a disinterested bystander. As C. Westermann has emphasized, the laments move on to petition and finally to praise.[7] They are protestations rooted in the power of our God to intervene. There is also the atmosphere of expectation, viz., that our God will hear and act on our behalf.[8]

The laments are a powerful demonstration of the centrality of covenant. Because of the triangular nature of cove-

[4]On the prayer dimension of the laments the following studies by W. Brueggemann are significant: "From Hurt to Joy, From Death to Life," *Int* 28 (1974) 3-19; "The Formfulness of Grief," *Int* 31 (1977) 263-274.

[5]Because of the preponderance of laments in the Psalter this chapter will study ten such psalms. The first five are individual laments, the second five are communal laments.

[6]Lament as used in the Psalms actually means complaint. By complaining and not lamenting, Israel hopes that her prayer will be heard. Speaking of Jeremiah's Confessions E. Gerstenberger ("Jeremiah's Complaints," *JBL* 82 [1963] 405, # 50) makes this useful distinction: a lament "bemoans a tragedy which cannot be reversed while a complaint entreats God for help in the midst of tribulation."

[7]See C. Westermann, *Praise and Lament*, 72-75.

[8]On the dimension of hope in the laments see E. Gerstenberger, "Der klagende Mensch," *Probleme biblischer Theologie: Gerhard von Rad zum 70. Geburtstag* (ed. H. W. Wolff; Munich: Kaiser, 1971) 64-72; (with W. Schrage) *Suffering* (Biblical Encounter Series; Nashville: Abingdon, 1980) 130-135.

nant (Yahweh, the community, and the individual) Yahweh
has a claim on us both as individuals and members of the
community. However, the other side is that we also have a
claim on Yahweh both as individuals and members of the
community. This covenant reality helps to explain the element of boldness that is so characteristic of these psalms
(see, e.g., Pss 44:23; 88:13-14). Because of the nature of
covenant we have the right to complain to this God and ask
for a hearing.

Yahweh thus becomes the God of my/our problem. What
the laments really presuppose is that my/our problem
necessarily becomes God's problem. The God of the covenant is not a dropout from our fragile human world. Unlike
the god of the deists, Yahweh continues to have a vested
interest in us and thus remains the committed covenant
partner. The God of my/our problem means the death of
solitude and isolation. We are linked to Another.[9]

Yahweh's problem also becomes my/our problem. The
other dimension of covenant is that Yahweh's problem, viz.,
other people, necessarily becomes my problem and/or the
problem of the community. When others are in disorientation, our God is in disorientation and hence must appeal to
us. The covenant nature of our relationship, the "we" setting
of cultic prayer, and the community orientation of Jeremiah's complaints[10] are powerful proofs for the involvement of
the individual and/or community in the needs and frustrations of others. The laments continue to be an eloquent
appeal to "get involved." We cannot pray to this God one-

---

[9] Lament is particularly significant in the liberation experience of the Exodus.
See J. Plastaras, *The God of Exodus* (Milwaukee: Bruce, 1966) 49-59.

[10] These Confessions of Jeremiah include the following texts: Jer 11:18-23;
12:1-6; 15:10-21; 17:12-18; 18:18-23; 20:7-13,14-18. Even if these texts do not
provide any biographical material about Jeremiah but are later theological reflections occasioned by the exile, they still indicate the community aspect of the
laments. For a brief survey of the pertinent literature see J. F. Craghan, *Love and
Thunder*, 137-139; J. L. Crenshaw, "A Living Tradition — The Book of Jeremiah
in Current Research," *Int* 37 (1983) 123-124; W. Brueggemann, "The Book of
Jeremiah - Portrait of the Prophet," ibid., 133-134.

on-one. To know Yahweh in prayer is also to be aware of Yahweh's extended family in their needs.

The laments admit different degrees of acceptance or denial. They speak of people who are just beginning to break free of their dependence on the old securities as well as of those who have accepted their demise as the springboard for reorientation.[11] Hence these prayers do not represent an overall artificial pattern whereby the psalmists refer to only one plateau in the process of disorientation. The laments are as large as life and reflect a spectrum moving from the tenacious grasp of the old to the loving acceptance of the new. Thus the psalms are prayers for all seasons.

Both the individual and communal laments evince the following basic structure: (a) address with an introductory cry for help; (b) lament; (c) confession of trust or assurance of being heard; (d) petition; (e) vow of praise.[12] A considerable problem is the explanation of the transition between distress and relief. A common view is that a cultic official pronounces an oracle of salvation which resolves the problem posed by the petitioner.[13] However, this view is being challenged more and more.[14] Despite the variance of scholarly opinion W. Brueggemann duly notes:

> "The question of how the changed mood and changed situation is effected cannot be definitively answered, but that it was changed is beyond doubt. And that is a central

---

[11] Psalm 88 is the only psalm in the Psalter which does not get beyond disorientation. See W. Brueggemann, "Psalms and the Life of Faith," 8-9, 14.

[12] See C. Westermann, *Praise and Lament*, 52-64; also "The Structure and History of the Lament in the Old Testament," ibid., 170.

[13] See J. Begrich, "Das priesterliche Heilsorakel," *ZAW* 52 (1934) 81-92. C. Westermann has followed Begrich's view. See his "The Way of the Promise Through the Old Testament," *The Old Testament and Christian Faith* (ed. B. W. Anderson; New York: Harper & Row, 1969) 202-205.

[14] Among such challengers see R. Kilian, "Ps 22 und das priesterliche Heilsorakel," *Biblische Zeitschrift* 12 (1968) 172-185; T. M. Raitt, *A Theology of Exile: Judgment/Deliverance in Jeremiah and Ezekiel* (Philadelphia: Fortress, 1977) 152-158. For a convenient summary of the various positions on this problem see W. Brueggemann, "From Hurt to Joy, From Death to Life," 9-10; "The Formfulness of Grief," 264.

conviction of Israel about the structure of reality. Life is transformed, health is restored, enemies are resisted and destroyed, death is averted, *shalom* is given again. The structure of the poem expresses this change. [15]

Psalm 3 [16]

> O Lord, how many are my foes!
> Many are rising against me;
> [2]many are saying of me,
>> there is no help for him in God.
>
>> *Selah*
>
> [3]But thou, O LORD, art a shield about me,
>> my glory, and the lifter of my head.
> [4]I cry aloud to the LORD
>> and he answers me from his holy hill.
>
>> *Selah*
>
> [5]I lie down and sleep;
>> I wake again, for the LORD sustains me.
> [6]I am not afraid of ten thousands of people
>> who have set themselves against
>> me round about.
>
> [7]Arise, O LORD!
>> Deliver me, O my God!
> For thou dost smite all my enemies on the cheek,
>> thou dost break the teeth of the wicked.
> [8]Deliverance belongs to the LORD;
>> thy blessing be upon thy people!
>
>> *Selah*

This psalm may be divided as follows: (a) appeal and lament (vv 1-2); (b) trust (vv 3-6); (c) petition (v 7); (d) vow of praise (v 8). L. Alonso Schökel notes three characters in the psalm: Yahweh, the psalmist, and the enemies. [17] The

[15] W. Brueggemann, "From Hurt to Joy, From Death to Life," 9-10.

[16] See A. Weiser, *The Psalms*, 116-119; H. –J. Kraus, *Psalmen*, 23-29.

[17] L. Alonso Schökel, *Treinta Salmos*, 54.

psalmist sees himself surrounded by a multitude of soldiers who are ready to attack him (v 1). It is their contention that Yahweh is incapable of saving him (v 2). However, Yahweh as the Divine Warrior[18] stands between the psalmist and the vast enemy force. His intervention is perhaps best reflected by translating verse 3: "But thou, Yahweh, art my sovereign, my glorious one who grants me the victory."[19] The psalmist continues this expression of faith by observing in verse 4 that Yahweh answers him from his holy mountain when he cries. This expression is the precise opposite of the enemies' contention in verse 2, viz., that Yahweh will not intervene to save him.

Yahweh intervenes by way of action. It is fitting that the psalmist reserve this action for the end of the poem: Yahweh smites the enemies on the cheek and breaks their teeth (v 7). However, prior to describing this definitive action the psalmist is careful to underline the attitude of trust. Thus, when the enemy rises up to attack (v 1), the psalmist lies down to sleep (v 5) and eventually to wake up. Even in its most precarious moments life continues to operate according to its basic rhythm. Sleep, therefore, symbolizes the victory of life. The psalmist is certain that, when morning comes, the Divine Warrior will begin the combat whose inevitable outcome is victory for the suppliant (v 6).[20]

In this poem the psalmist clearly experiences disorientation. In the face of a huge and menacing army the harmony of life has disintegrated. However, the crisis (the military symbol is plastic enough to cover a variety of human predicaments) becomes a faith opportunity. The description of

[18] On the basic theology of the holy war see R. de Vaux, *Ancient Israel*, 258-267. On Yahweh as the Divine Warrior see P. D. Miller, "God the Warrior," *Int* 19 (1965) 39-46; *The Divine Warrior in Early Israel* (Harvard Semitic Monographs 5; Cambridge: Harvard University, 1973); F. M. Cross, *Canaanite Myth and Hebrew Epic*, 91-111. For an extensive bibliography on the topics of war, holy war, and Yahweh's war see N. Lohfink (ed.), *Gewalt und Gewaltlosigkeit im Alten Testament*, 236-238.

[19] See M. Dahood, *Psalms 1-50*, 16-18.

[20] See L. Alonso Schökel, *Treinta Salmos*, 56.

confidence which culminates in sleep suggest that he has been willing to let go and accept the intervention of his God. Hence disorientation will not be the last word. The darkness is not insuperable. The day is dawning, the moment when the Divine Warrior will definitively intervene.

At prayer we cannot dismiss the shocks in our lives. Indeed they are so real that they appear to impinge on the harmony of our prayer. However, the appearance is deceiving because such shocks rightly become the raw material of prayer. To find healing, we must turn to Another who does not regard our woes as trivial but as the stuff out of which we can grow. Without dismissing human effort, this psalm emphasizes the fact that we cannot resolve all problems by ourselves. We must learn to lean upon Another and see that dependence, not as the loss of autonomy, but as the growth of our relationship. In the other direction this psalm challenges us to be the Divine Warrior for others. The implication of this title, viz., concern for one's people at critical moments, is imposed on us by reason of covenant. At prayer we must not cease to picture our God as beset by worries and afflicted with pain. Our God's worries and afflictions (other people) become ours. The disturbing question is: will at least some of God's people sleep tonight because we have committed ourselves to action in the morning?

Psalm 22[21]

> My God, my God, why hast thou forsaken me?
>> Why are thou so far from helping me, from the words of my groaning?
> [2]O my God, I cry by day, but thou dost not answer;
>> and by night, but find no rest.
>
> [3]Yet thou art holy,
>> enthroned on the praises of Israel.

---

[21]See A. Weiser, *The Psalms*, 217-226; H. - J. Kraus, *Psalmen*, 174-185; S. Terrien, *The Elusive Presence*, 321-323; C. Westermann, *Praise and Lament*, 68-69.

⁴In thee our fathers trusted;
    they trusted, and thou didst deliver them.
⁵To thee they cried, and were saved;
    in thee they trusted, and were not disappointed.

⁶But I am a worm, and no man;
    scorned by men, and despised by the people.
⁷All who see me mock at me,
    they make mouths at me, they wag their heads;
⁸"He committed his cause to the LORD;
    let him deliver him,
let him rescue him, for he delights in him!"

⁹Yet thou art he who took me from the womb;
    thou didst keep me safe upon my mother's breasts.
¹⁰Upon thee was I cast from my birth,
    and since my mother bore me thou hast been my God.

¹¹Be not far from me,
    for trouble is near
    and there is none to help.

¹²Many bulls encompass me,
    strong bulls of Bashan surround me;
¹³they open wide their mouths at me,
    like a ravening and roaring lion.
¹⁴I am poured out like water,
  and all my bones are out of joint;
my heart is like wax,
    it is melted within my breast;
¹⁵my strength is dried up like a potsherd,
    and my tongue cleaves to my jaws;
    thou dost lay me in the dust of death.

¹⁶Yea, dogs are round about me;
    a company of evildoers encircle me;
    they have pierced my hands and feet—
¹⁷I can count all my bones—
    they stare and gloat over me;
¹⁸they divide my garments among them,

and for my raiment they cast lots.
[19]But thou, O LORD, be not far off!
O thou my help, hasten to my aid!
[20]Deliver my soul from the sword,
my life from the power of the dog!
[20]Save me from the mouth of the lion,
my afflicted soul from the horns of the wild oxen!

[22]I will tell of thy name to my brethren;
in the midst of the congregation I will praise thee:
[23]You who fear the LORD, praise him!
all you sons of Jacob, glorify him,
and stand in awe of him, all you sons of Israel!
[24]For he has not despised or abhorred
the affliction of the afflicted;
and he has not hid his face from him,
but he has heard, when he cried to him.
[25]From thee comes my praise in the great congregation;
my vows I will pay before those who fear him.

[26]The afflicted shall eat and be satisfied;
those who seek him shall praise the LORD!
May your hearts live for ever!

[27]All the ends of the earth shall remember
and turn to the LORD;
and all the families of the nations
shall worship before him.
[28]For dominion belongs to the LORD
and he rules over the nations.

[29]Yea, to him shall all the proud of the earth bow down;
before him shall bow all who go down to the dust,
and he who cannot keep himself alive.
[30]Posterity shall serve him;
men shall tell of the Lord to the coming generation,
[31]and proclaim his deliverance to a people yet unborn,
that he has wrought it.

This psalm is certainly one of the most moving in the entire Psalter. It combines utter frustration and dereliction with a sustained hope in the God of Israel. In the midst of life's greatest crisis there is the incessant search for divine presence. The psalmist who is seriously ill and abandoned by all (perhaps imprisoned as well) finds not only his life unintelligible but also his God unbending. As C. Stuhlmueller puts it, the poem revolves around the deaf and silent God:

> "If we combine the paradoxical contrast of vv 2-3 of roaring outcry and oppressive silence, we find the psalmist so isolated that no one can hear even his shrieks of dismay. We are reminded of the philosophical discussion: does a tree, crashing to the ground, make any sound if no one is present to hear it? The key dilemma then is the absent, silent, deaf God!"[22]

The original psalm consists of verses 1-21 (lament) and verses 22-26 (thanksgiving). The lament may be divided as follows: (a) invocation and cry for help (vv 1-2); (b) motivation (vv 3-5); (c) lament (vv 6-8); (d) expression of confidence (vv 9-10); (e) prayer for help (v 11); (f) lament (vv 12-18); (g) prayer for help (vv 19-21). In verses 22-26 the psalmist celebrates a thanksgiving liturgy. He fulfills his vows (v 25) while those joining him share in a meal (v 26). In keeping with the theme of the lament proper there is the profession that Yahweh has indeed heard (v 24). Verses 27-31 are an expansion of the original thanksgiving. At a later date another member of God's community (v 25) extended the poem to include the Gentiles (vv 27-28), the sick and perhaps the dead (v 29),[23] and the unborn (v 31).

---

[22] C. Stuhlmueller, "Psalm 22: The Deaf and Silent God of Mysticism and Liturgy," *BTB* 12 (1982) 88.

[23] See M. Dahood, *Psalms 1-50*, 138, 144.

The psalmist in verses 1-21 is utterly innocent. He does not recite any previous sins. He does not inveigh against his enemies. Nonetheless he suffers. That suffering is depicted in symbols borrowed from the animal world: worm (v 6), bulls (v 13), dogs (vv 16,20), lion and wild oxen (v 21). It also finds expression in images describing his bodily condition: poured out like water with disjointed bones (v 14), heart like wax (v 15), strength (or possibly throat) dried up like a potsherd and tongue clinging to the jaws (v 15). The attitude of the people is hardly reassuring. They ridicule the psalmist since his condition must reflect sin (vv 6-8). They merely look on and gloat (v 17), they anticipate the moment of death (v 18).[24]

Interspersed are the protestations of confidence. Particularly noteworthy is the record of Yahweh's previous interventions. Earlier generations were in straits yet God did not abandon them. They were delivered and saved (vv 4-5). However, the pain mounts in the setting of silence. As Yahweh is seated on his throne in the sanctuary ready to accede to the needs of his people (v 3), the only sound is deafening silence. "The God of the liturgy turns out to be deaf!"[25]

Stuhlmueller has made a strong case for seeing the poignancy and depth of the lament in the inclusion formed by verses 1-2 and 19-21. In verse 1 Yahweh is *far* from the psalmist and in verse 19 he prays that his God be not *far* off (see also verse 11). In verse 1 Yahweh is far from *saving* the psalmist (translated "helping" in RSV) but in verse 21 the poet calls upon Yahweh to *save* him. In verse 2 despite the incessant cries of the psalmist Yahweh does not *hear*. Yet in verse 21 comes the statement: "You have *heard* me!"[26] In the light of this inclusion there is a movement from the deaf and seemingly unbending God to a Yahweh who is now "all

---

[24] See N. Lohfink, "On the Enemies of the Sick," 159-161.

[25] C. Stuhlmueller, "Psalm 22," 89.

[26] Ibid., 87. RSV indicates in a footnote that the Hebrew text of verse 21 reads "thou hast answered me" rather than "my afflicted soul."

ears." According to this view the task of the psalmist is to secure an audience with Yahweh. It is not surprising that the thanksgiving begins immediately in verse 22.

At prayer we must ponder the price of commitment which is so often the source of disorientation. According to verse 8 the psalmist's life is bound up with his God — something that should result in reorientation according to the poet's scoffers. Instead of the quick and decisive movement to reorientation that we crave (v 22), we may often hear the penetrating sound of silence. We naturally pose this question because of the impasse: is it reasonable to continue to trust? We are tempted to think that the Faithful One is more responsive to infidelity.

In the face of such inexplicable forces we are encouraged to cling to a person. Our life must still be grounded in a Thou. This God is still *my* God (vv 1-2). "Yet *thou* art he who took *me* from the womb;... Upon *thee* was *I* cast from my birth..." (vv 9-10).

At prayer we are perhaps challenged to a great extent in assuming the place of the deaf God. To those who do not hear encouragement and hope from their God we are asked to be present and listen. So often ours is not the task to offer rational explanations of seemingly irrational divine aberrations. Ours is the task to provide the ministry of listening. Ours is the task to offer the ministry of presence. Whenever one human listens to another distraught human, the One "enthroned on the praises of Israel" (v 3) is present. Prayer thus becomes the occasion for bending God's ear in another direction.

Psalm 39[27]

> I said, "I will guard my ways,
>   that I may not sin with my tongue;
> I will bridle my mouth,
>   so long as the wicked are in my presence."

[27] See A. Weiser, *The Psalms*, 326-331; H.-J. Kraus, *Psalmen*, 299-304.

²I was dumb and silent,
   I held my peace to no avail;
  my distress grew worse,
³my heart became hot within me.
  As I mused, the fire burned;
      then I spoke with my tongue:

⁴"LORD, let me know my end,
      and what is the measure of my days;
      let me know how fleeting my life is!
⁵Behold, thou hast made my days a few handbreadths,
      and my lifetime is as nothing in thy sight.
  Surely every man stands as a mere breath!

                                                     Selah

⁶Surely man goes about as a shadow!
  Surely for nought are they in turmoil;
      man heaps up, and knows not who will gather!
⁷"And now, Lord, for what do I wait?
      My hope is in thee.
⁸Deliver me from all my transgressions.
  Make me not the scorn of the fool!

⁹I am dumb, I do not open my mouth;
      for it is thou who hast done it.
¹⁰Remove thy stroke from me;
      I am spent by the blows of thy hand.
¹¹When thou dost chasten man with rebukes for sin,
      thou dost consume like a moth what is dear to him;
      surely every man is a mere breath!

                                                     Selah

¹²"Hear my prayer, O LORD,
      and give ear to my cry;
      hold not thy peace at my tears!
  For I am thy passing guest,
      a sojourner, like all my fathers.

¹³Look away from me, that I may know gladness,
      before I depart and be no more!"

This psalm is ultimately a study on the theology of security, a meditation on the irony of human experience vis-à-vis the Existing One. Thus in light of the transitory and fleeting nature of life the basis of human confidence is not a thing, a principle, a system. It is a person, viz., Yahweh. The poem may be divided as follows: (a) introduction which hammers home the conviction that silence is simply inadequate (vv 1-3); (b) the impermanence of human existence (vv 4-7); (c) petition for deliverance (vv 8-11); (d) supplication for the hearing of the petition (vv 12-13).

The psalmist has apparently been the object of ridicule and verbal abuse because of his religious convictions. Hence he resolved to curb his mouth (vv 1-2) rather than lash out against his opponents. However, the resolution did not work. The psalmist's condition became all the more precarious as he vainly attempted to refrain from speaking out (vv 3-4). The silence was hardly golden!

Instead of asking for the overthrow of his assailants, the poet now proceeds to reflect on the human condition after the manner of the wisdom tradition. After requesting knowledge of his own fleeting life (v 4), the psalmist muses on the meaning of human life as such, not his personal afflictions. Humans stand as a mere *breath* (v 5 — *hebel* in Hebrew) and wander as a shadow (v 6). *Hebel* has to do with irony, i.e., the perception of the distance between pretense and reality.[28] In the style of Ecclesiastes (see Eccl 6:2,12) one must conclude that the one who heaps up will not necessarily gather. The plight of the psalmist is now ironically linked to human existence as such.

In verses 8-11 the psalmist asks for deliverance. He seeks divine help in a situation where humans are only *hebel* (v 11). Despite the vicious circle of human existence he finds

---

[28] On the translation of *hebel* as "irony" especially in Ecclesiastes see E. M. Good, *Irony in the Old Testament* (Philadelphia: Westminster, 1965) 168-195; T. Polk, "The Wisdom of Irony: A Study of *Hebel* and Its Relation to Joy and the Fear of God in Ecclesiastes," *Studia Biblica et Theologica* 6, #1 (March, 1976) 3-17.

hope in a person, Yahweh (v 7). In the words of W. A. M. Beuken:

> "Now that all earthly support has been undermined, only two choices are left: to turn away from the power which has made human life such as it is, or to turn to it and surrender. The psalmist chooses the latter. He goes searching for a personal God, sensitive to his short lifetime and willing to have pity on him. The step which he takes from his distress, accidental as it is, is not to a God whom he asks to restore his previous thoughtless and carefree existence, but to a God whom he accepts as having made human existence itself distressful."[29]

In his supplication (vv 12-13), which one would expect before verse 7 or 8, the psalmist seeks deliverance from his present predicament (vv 12a, 13a). However, the motive for Yahweh's intervention is the human condition itself. A sojourner (v 12b) was a permanent resident with certain privileges but still incapable of owning land. A lodger (v 12b) enjoyed less stability than a sojourner.[30] As Beuken suggests,[31] this was the condition of the patriarchs, viz., dwelling in the land but not yet possessing it. Whereas a form of immortality was present in the continuation of one's family on the land, the psalmist concludes that the reality of the human condition is not the security of owning land but the security of depending on Yahweh. While this is not an afterlife in terms of resurrection of the body and/or immortality of the soul, it does contain the seed of the afterlife — rootedness in the covenant God.

At prayer we cannot avoid the question of values which is

[29] W. A. M. Beuken, "Psalm 39: Some Aspects of the Old Testament Understanding of Prayer," *Heythrop Journal* 19 (1978) 3.

[30] On the notion of sojourner and lodger see R. de Vaux, *Ancient Israel*, 74-76.

[31] W. A. M. Beuken, "Psalm 39," 7. On the centrality of responsibility in these traditions see W. Brueggemann, *The Land: Place as Gift, Promise, and Challenge in Biblical Faith* (Overtures to Biblical Theology; Philadelphia: Fortress, 1977) 59-67.

so often at the bottom of our disorientation. What makes
life congruous or incongruous? What overcomes the *hebel*
or irony we experience? We must truly inquire whether or
not we merely tabulate our meritorious actions and so
denigrate our God to the level of the Celestial Administra-
tor. At prayer we must seek to encounter a God who is not
the fiction of our virtuous deeds but the bedrock of our daily
existence. As we seek to address our disorientation, we must
make the strategic move from things to person: "'And now,
Lord, for *what* do I wait? My hope is in *thee*'" (v 7).

In the other direction we must offer person-oriented hope
to the distraught of our world. Because of covenant we are
to be sources of confidence, weak and fickle though we
sometimes are! To those who find human existence drab
and meaningless, we are to offer a new vision of life rooted
in the Living One. Prayer is the catalyst for making our hope
the patrimony of others, so that sojourners and lodgers may
become full-fledged citizens.

Psalm 42-43[32]

> As a hart longs
>   for flowing streams,
> so longs my soul
>   for thee, O God.
> [2]My soul thirsts for God,
>   for the living God.
> When shall I come and behold
>   the face of God?
> [3]My tears have been my food
>   day and night,
> while men say to me continually,
>   "Where is your God?"
> [4]These things I remember,
>   as I pour out my soul:

[32]See A. Weiser, *The Psalms*, 346-352;   H. –J. Kraus, *Psalmen*, 316-322; E.
Haag, "Die Sehnsucht nach dem lebendigen Gott im Zeugnis des Psalms 42/43,"
Geist und Leben 49 (1976) 167-177.

how I went with the throng,
    and led them in procession to the house of God,
with glad shouts and songs of thanksgiving,
    a multitude keeping festival.
[5]Why are you cast down, O my soul,
    and why are you disquieted within me?
Hope in God; for I shall again praise him,
    my help [6]and my God.
My soul is cast down within me,
    therefore I remember thee
from the land of Jordan and of Hermon,
    from Mount Mizar.
[7]Deep calls to deep
    at the thunder of thy cataracts;
all thy waves and thy billows
    have gone over me.
[8]By day the LORD commands his steadfast love;
    and at night his song is with me,
    a prayer to the God of my life.

[9]I say to God, my rock:
    "Why hast thou forgotten me?
Why go I mourning
    because of the oppression of the enemy?"
[10]As with a deadly wound in my body,
    my adversaries taunt me,
while they say to me continually,
    "Where is your God?"

[11]Why are you cast down, O my soul,
    and why are you disquieted within me?
Hope in God; for I shall again praise him,
    my help and my God.

Vindicate me, O God, and defend my cause
    against an ungodly people;
from deceitful and unjust men deliver me!
[2]For thou art the God in whom I take refuge;
    why hast thou cast me off?

Why go I mourning
because of the oppression of the enemy?

³Oh send out thy light and thy truth;
   let them lead me,
let them bring me to thy holy hill
   and to thy dwelling!
⁴Then I will go to the altar of God,
   to God my exceeding joy;
and I will praise thee with the lyre,
   O God, my God.

⁵Why are you cast down, O my soul,
   and why are you disquieted within me?
Hope in God; for I shall again praise him,
   my help and my God.

These two psalms were originally a single poem. An indication of this is that the refrain of 42:11 is repeated in 43:2 and the refrain of 42:6,11 is likewise repeated in 43:5. In Alonso Schökel's poetic analysis[33] there are three strophes (42:1-5; 42:6-11; 43:1-5), each of which concludes with the refrain: "Why are you cast down, O my soul, and why are you disquieted within me? Hope in God; for I shall again praise him, my help and my God." There are two major images: (a) water as life (strophe #1); and (b) water as death (strophe #2).

The psalmist is the object of ridicule because of his reliance on Yahweh (see 42:3,10; 43:1). He suffers from the absence of God, although the precise cause (sickness, persecution, etc.) is not pinpointed. He finds himself in a mountainous area south of Mount Hermon where he sees a deer desperately searching for water (42:1a). The psalmist then

---

[33]L. Alonso Schökel, *Treinta Salmos*, 147-165. An earlier version of this analysis appeared in English: "The Poetic Structure of Psalm 42-43," *JSOT* 1 (1976) 4-11. This English article was accompanied by two responses: M. Kessler, "Response," ibid., 12-15; N. H. Ridderbos, "Response," ibid., 16-21. In turn, Alonso Schökel replied to his respondents: "Psalm 42-43: A Response to Ridderbos and Kessler," *JSOT* 3 (1977) 61-65.

projects his experience into the image of the deer (42:1b-2). The poet's whole being ("my soul") is now devoured by an animal thirst for God. In this same area (close by the sources of the Jordan — see 43:6) he also experiences the thundering torrents which remind him of the chaos associated with the primeval ocean. Here the water is not life-giving — it is destructive (42:8). This tension is finally resolved by the minor image of light and fidelity in the third strophe (43:3).

The transition from disorientation to reorientation takes place in an inner dialogue. On one level of consciousness nostalgia and dismay predominate as the psalmist experiences the absence of God by recalling the temple liturgy (42:4). On another level of consciousness confidence and hope grow as the poet anticipates the presence of God, viz., light and fidelity bringing him to God's dwelling place (43:3). The key problem is the absence of God. As Alonso Schökel notes:

> "The manner of God's presence is awareness of his absence. Absence which is not noticed nor deeply felt is a simple absence which causes no grief. But absence which is felt is a means of being present in the consciousness, bringing anxiety and grief. Paradoxically, the taunts of the enemies sharpen the sensation of God's absence and thus, in the form of nostalgia, increase the sense of his presence."[34]

The transition from disorientation to reorientation is observable in other ways. In the area of liturgy there is the dramatic movement from past nostalgia for worship (42:4) to future participation in divine services (43:4). In the area of time there is the decided switch from the painful succession of day and night where tears are the psalmist's food (42:3) to the optimistic rhythm of day and night where his God's covenant fidelity is linked to praise (42:8). In the

---

[34] L. Alonso Schökel, "The Poetic Structure of Psalm 42-43," 8-9.

nuances of the chief refrain there is noticeable transformation. In 42:5 the voice is timid and stifled. In 42:11 it is affirmative and reproachful. In 43:5 it is triumphant and victorious.

At prayer we also yearn for a sign of God's presence, something concrete that will show that he is there. Deep within we acknowledge that our move from disorientation (death, disease, unemployment, falling out of love, rejection by friends, etc.) to reorientation is fundamentally our move from the absence to the presence of God. Prayer is that paradoxical moment when the disconcerting facts of our disorientation evoke past presences and make us press on for newer ones. Prayer is that occasion when the hope of the chief refrain of this psalm exhorts us to leave the old behind and accept the new. It is a time when we confess our limited human resources and thereby no longer hope in *them* but in our *God*. Reorientation is the embrace of the all-powerful God and the kiss goodbye to our ego-centered forces.

Presence makes the heart grow fonder. Because of covenant involvement we are called upon to make our experience of God's presence at prayer, especially at liturgy, the basis of hope for others. To know our God's presence in these settings is to be aware of our God's absence in other situations, viz., broken humans who long for presence but do not feel capable of even articulating that longing. Merely to stand beside an alienated human is to symbolize the contagious dimension of prayer. To hear the Word proclaimed and to share in Eucharist means to move from the sanctuary to the hospital, nursing home, jail, home, etc. Prayer is not the occasion for our egotistical hoarding of God's presence. Prayer is the moment for our altrustic overcoming of God's absence. Prayer is to be the assault on the disorientation of others whereby they will be moved to say: "Hope in God; for I shall again praise him, my help and my God."

Psalm 69[35]

> Save me, O God!
> For the waters have come up to my neck.
> [2]I sink in deep mire,
>> where there is no foothold;
> I have come into deep waters,
>> and the flood sweeps over me.
> [3]I am weary with my crying;
>> my throat is parched.
> My eyes grow dim
>> with waiting for my God.
> [4]More in number than the hairs of my head
>> are those who hate me without cause;
> mighty are those who would destroy me,
>> those who attack me with lies.
> What I did not steal must I now restore?
>
> [5]O God, thou knowest my folly;
>> the wrongs I have done are not hidden from thee.
>
> [6]Let not those who hope in thee be
>> put to shame through me,
>> O Lord GOD of hosts;
> let not those who seek thee be
>> brought to dishonor through me,
>> O God of Israel.
> [7]For it is for thy sake that I have borne reproach,
>> that shame has covered my face.
> [8]I have become a stranger to my brethren,
>> an alien to my mother's sons.
> [9]For zeal for thy house has consumed me,
>> and the insults of those who insult
>> thee have fallen on me.
> [10]When I humbled my soul with fasting,
>> it became my reproach.

[35]See A. Weiser, *The Psalms*, 490-495; H. –J. Kraus, *Psalmen*, 478-485. For the use of Psalm 69 in the New Testament see H. –J. Kraus, *Theologie der Psalmen*, 241-243; C. Stuhlmueller, *Psalms*, 1. 311-312.

[11]When I made sackcloth my clothing,
   I became a byword to them.
[12]I am the talk of those who sit in the gate,
   and the drunkards make songs about me.
[13]But as for me, my prayer is to thee, O LORD.
   At an acceptable time, O God,
      in the abundance of thy steadfast love answer me.
   With thy faithful help [14]rescue me
      from sinking in the mire;
   let me be delivered from my enemies
      and from the deep waters.
[15]Let not the flood sweep over me,
   or the deep swallow me up,
   or the pit close its mouth over me.
[16]Answer me, O LORD, for thy steadfast love is good;
   according to thy abundant mercy, turn to me.
[17]Hide not thy face from thy servant;
   for I am in distress, make haste to answer me.
[18]Draw near to me, redeem me,
   set me free because of my enemies!
[19]Thou knowest my reproach,
   and my shame and my dishonor;
   my foes are all known to thee.
[20]Insults have broken my heart,
   so that I am in despair.
   I looked for pity, but there was none;
   and for comforters, but I found none.
[21]They gave me poison for food,
   and for my thirst they gave me vinegar to drink.

[22]Let their own table before them become a snare;
   let their sacrificial feasts be a trap.
[23]Let their eyes be darkened, so that they cannot see;
   and make their loins tremble continually.
[24]Pour out thy indignation upon them,
   and let thy burning anger overtake them.
[25]May their camp be a desolation,
   let no one dwell in their tents.

²⁶For they persecute him whom thou hast smitten,
and him whom thou hast wounded, they afflict still
more.
²⁷Add to them punishment upon punishment;
may they have no acquittal from thee.
²⁸Let them be blotted out of the book of the living;
let them not be enrolled among the righteous.

²⁹But I am afflicted and in pain;
let thy salvation, O God, set me on high!
³⁰I will praise the name of God with a song;
I will magnify him with thanksgiving.
³¹This will please the LORD more than an ox
or a bull with horns and hoofs.
³²Let the oppressed see it and be glad;
you who seek God, let your hearts revive.
³³For the LORD hears the needy,
and does not despise his own that are in bonds.

³⁴Let heaven and earth praise him,
the seas and everything that moves therein.
³⁵For God will save Zion
and rebuild the cities of Judah;
and his servants shall dwell there and possess it;
³⁶the children of his servants shall inherit it,
and those who love his name shall dwell in it.

This lament is a graphic description of acute pain, faith in
Yahweh, and the desire for revenge. The psalmist is
seriously ill (vv 26,29), perhaps to the point of death (vv 1-2).
He is persecuted by enemies (v 4) and smitten by God (vv
8-9). The poem may be divided as follows: (a) cry for help (v
1a); (b) lament (vv 1b-4); (c) acknowledgement of wrongdo-
ing (v 5); (d) prayer (v 6); (e) lament (vv 7-12); (f) prayer (vv
13-18); (g) lament (vv 19-21); (h) curse against the enemy (vv
22-29); (i) thanksgiving (vv 30-34); (j) addition in the aftermath of the destruction of Jerusalem (vv 35-36).
    The poet paints a powerful picture of human dereliction.

In verses 1b-2 (note also verses 14-15) the psalmist depicts himself as being in Sheol, the underworld: deep waters, mire, flood. Sheol is more a state than a place. It is the state of being removed from God's concern and experiencing utter loneliness. Although the psalmist is not without sin (v 5), still the present debacle is senseless. Indeed it is scandalous. Yahweh's faithful people may be led to doubt their God because of the psalmist's unmitigated suffering (v 6). But the irony of the situation is that this catastrophe is the result of serving Yahweh. For Yahweh's sake he has borne reproach (v 7a), out of zeal for Yahweh's house he has known affliction (v 9a). The disheartening reality is that Yahweh is totally aware of his servant's condition (v 19), yet apparently does not even lift a finger to help. Perhaps the pathos of the poem reaches its highest point in verse 20b where the psalmist seeks pity and comfort only to find none.[36]

Verses 22-29, the psalmist's curse against the enemy, raise the problem of the cursing psalms in general and the significance of these verses for the psalmist in particular. In their approach to prayer not a few have recommended that these verses be eliminated from the church's official liturgical books or at least drastically truncated.[37] Such people are naturally appalled by these vehement expressions of revenge and question their relevancy for prayer. Two questions emerge: (a) what is the intent of these psalms? and (b) is there a place for anger in our prayer life?

Justice is the intent of these psalms. In the ancient Near East,[38] where police forces and correctional institutions

---

[36] On the expression "none to comfort" as related to Israel's traditions of the land see W. Brueggemann, *The Land*, 130-150.

[37] B. Ströle ("Psalmen — Lieder der Verfolgten." *BK* 35 1980 42-47), noting the problem of adapting these psalms to Christian prayer, concludes that it is better to "spiritualize" such passages rather than omit them. C. Hinricher ("Die Fluch — und Vergeltungspsalmen im Stundengebet," ibid., 55-59), a member of the religious community at Dachau, holds that certain psalms and verses of psalms cannot be prayed by that community.

[38] Against the background of power L. Ruppert ("Klagelieder in Israel und Babylonien — verschiedene Deutungen der Gewalt," *Gewalt und Gewaltlosigkeit im*

were non-existent, the curse played a prominent role in the human quest for justice. These curses were solemn legal formulae. They were considered legally binding and rested on the sanction of the deity upon whose will the entire social order depended. Essentially they were powerful demands that justice prevail by means of divine intervention:

> "This means that these imprecations were, in fact, for the poor man fighting his battle for faith in an almost total darkness, a prayer for God to show his hand, vindicate the social order which was part of his own divine order and bring redress.[39]

Anger occupies a legitimate place in our prayer life.[40] Too often we have been seduced by Stoicism into thinking that emotion opposes reason. According to Israel's traditions the emotion evidenced by the lament of the Hebrews (see Ex 2:6) is the reaction that moves Yahweh to act on behalf of his people. According to sound psychology we must reply to life's threats through anger. Anger thereby becomes a significant component in our human growth. To suppress anger

Alten Testament, 111-158) has compared the Babylonian and Israelite laments. First, whereas the Babylonian laments concentrate almost entirely on bodily sickness, the Israelite laments deal more with interhuman relationships which have degenerated into rivalry. Second, whereas in Babylonia the cause of oppression is almost exclusively demons (and hence magicians and sorcerers unknown to the petitioner), in Israel the cause is bound up, on the one hand, with disturbed social relationships and, on the other hand, with the wrath of Yahweh. Third, whereas in Babylonia the petitioner not only seeks the help of the deities in ritual but also takes an active part in magic and the destruction of the opposing forces, in Israel the petitioner leaves the situation entirely up to God and expects everything from him.

[39] J. Blenkinsopp, "Can we Pray the Cursing Psalms?" *A Sketchbook of Biblical Theology*, 85. This study appeared earlier in slightly different form in: *Clergy Review* 50 (1965) 534-538. It is useful to recall that in Deuteronomy 28 the entire Israelite community invokes a long list of curses on itself in the event that it is unfaithful to the terms of the covenant. The curses, therefore, are a profound expression of their covenant allegiance.

[40] See S. Carney, "God Damn God: A Reflection on Expressing Anger in Prayer," *BTB* 13 (1983) 116-120.

does not contribute to an integral human life.[41] According to covenant theology God's people have the right to articulate their grief in a community setting. The destructive tendencies of social evil are expressed in a forum where the sufferers can hope for the bottoming out of disorientation. Ultimately anger does not necessarily stifle the human spirit since it is capable of rendering us yet more human.[42]

At prayer we dare not hide or suppress the grief that overwhelms us. In seeking to move from disorientation to reorientation we are encouraged after the manner of Psalm 69 not only to speak out but also to become angry. Our predecessors in the chronological and ascending order are Moses, Jeremiah, and Jesus.[43] No one would suggest that their prayer was faulty. No one would infer that their prayer was disrespectful. In communing with this same God we are urged to follow these intrepid examples of biblical tradition. Our is not a God who advises that we utter only churchy prayers. Ours is not a God who recommends that we speak the polite language of manuals of devotion. Ours is a God who wants his presence recognized even if the only way of acknowledging that presence is the raw speech of angry laments.[44]

---

[41] See A. D. Lester, "Toward a New Understanding of Anger in Christian Experience," *Review and Expositor* 78 (1981) 563-590.

[42] C. S. Lewis (*Reflections on the Psalms*, 33) notes: "Against all this the ferocious parts of the Psalms serve as a reminder that there is in the world such a thing as wickedness and that it (if not its perpetrators) is hateful to God."

[43] For Jeremiah and his Confessions see below, #10. For Jesus and his use of Psalm 22 in the gospels see the reflections on Mk 15:21-39 at the end of this chapter. For Moses the following texts are significant: Ex 15:22—17:7; 32:1—34:35; Num 11:1-12:16; 14:1-45; 16:1-50; 20:2-13; 21:4-9. On these traditions see G. W. Coats, *Rebellion in the Wilderness: The Murmuring Motif in the Wilderness Traditions of the Old Testament* (Nashville: Abingdon, 1968); "The King's Loyal Opposition: Obedience: and Authority in Exodus 32-34," *Canon and Authority* (ed. G. W. Coats & B. O. Long; Philadelphia: Fortress, 1977) 91-109. See also S. H. Blank, "Men Against God: The Promethean Element in Biblical Prayer," *JBL* 72 (1953) 1-13.

[44] In *The Town Beyond the Wall* (New York: Avon, 1969, 123) E. Wiesel has Michael speak to Pedro after the manner of these laments: "'I want to blaspheme, and I can't quite manage it. I go up against Him. I shake my fist, I froth with rage, but it's still a way of telling Him that He's there, that He exists, that He's never the

At prayer, even our most intimate prayer, we must hear the laments of others who are empowered to overcome our insensitivity by their rightful demand for social justice. We are challenged by this psalm to undo the plight of the psalmist for our audience. We are asked to comfort the comfortless and pity the pitiless (see verse 20). We are furthermore challenged to bring to public attention the anger that has been suppressed and the anxiety that has been denied.[45] Prayer must mean that the unexpressed fears and frustrations of fellow humans will come to the surface so that brothers and sisters will no longer sink in the deep mire (vv 2,14) or be overwhelmed by the deep waters (vv 2,14). By such prayer we will understand the angry Jesus who pronounced curses on those who did not provide for the hungry, the thirsty, the strangers, the naked, and the imprisoned (see Matt 25:41-45).

Psalm 44[46]

> We have heard with our ears, O God,
> > our fathers have told us,
> what deeds thou didst perform in their days,
> > in the days of old:
> [2]thou with thy own hand didst drive out the nations,
> > but them thou didst plant;
> thou didst afflict the peoples,
> > but them thou didst set free;
> [3]for not by their own sword did they win the land,
> > not did their own arm give them victory;
> but thy right hand, and thy arm,
> > and the light of thy countenance;
> > for thou didst delight in them.

same twice, that denial itself is an offering to his grandeur. The shout becomes a prayer in spite of me.'"

[45] On this prophetic role see W. Brueggemann, *The Prophetic Imagination* (Philadelphia: Fortress, 1978) 49-51.

[46] See A. Weiser, *The Psalms*, 352-360; H.–J. Kraus, *Psalmen*, 323-329.

⁴Thou art my King and my God,
    who ordainest victories for Jacob.
⁵Through thee we push down our foes;
    through thy name we tread down our assailants.
⁶For not in my bow do I trust,
    nor can my sword save me.
⁷But thou hast saved us from our foes,
    and hast put to confusion those who hate us.
⁸In God we have boasted continually,
    and we will give thanks to thy name for ever.

Selah

⁹Yet thou hast cast us off and abased us,
    and hast not gone out with our armies.
¹⁰Thou hast made us turn back from the foe;
    and our enemies have gotten spoil.
¹¹Thou hast made us like sheep for slaughter,
    and hast scattered us among the nations.
¹²Thou hast sold thy people for a trifle,
    demanding no high price for them.

¹³Thou hast made us the taunt of our neighbors,
    the derision and scorn of those about us.
¹⁴Thou hast made us a byword among the nations,
    a laughingstock among the peoples.
¹⁵All day long my disgrace is before me,
    and shame has covered my face,
¹⁶at the words of the taunters and revilers,
    at the sight of the enemy and the avenger.

¹⁷All this has come upon us,
    though we have not forgotten thee,
    or been false to thy covenant.
¹⁸Our heart has not turned back,
    nor have our steps departed from thy way,
¹⁹that thou shouldst have broken us in the place of jackals,
    and covered us with deep darkness.

20If we had forgotten the name of our God,
or spread forth our hands to a strange god,
21would not God discover this?
For he knows the secrets of the heart.
22Nay, for thy sake we are slain all the day long,
and accounted as sheep for the slaughter.

23Rouse thyself! Why sleepest thou, O Lord!
Awake! Do not cast us off for ever!
24Why dost thou hide thy face?
Why dost thou forget our affliction and oppression?
25For our soul is bowed down to the dust;
our body cleaves to the ground.
26Rise up, come to our help!
Deliver us for the sake of thy steadfast love!

In this communal lament Israel probes the apparent absence of her God. The distance between her creedal formulations of Yahweh's fidelity and the present state of affairs threatens to become an ever widening chasm with theology on one side and history on the other. The psalm reflects some national catastrophe, although one cannot be more specific as to the precise event.[47] In the Psalter the psalm transcends its original setting to offer a paradigm for coping with Yahweh's apparent aloofness. It may be divided as follows: (a) recitation of Yahweh's past record of fidelity (vv 1-3); (b) trust as Israel's expected response (vv 4-8); (c) a vivid description of the present impasse (vv 9-16); (d) protestations of fidelity and trust (vv 17-22); (e) a bold demand for Yahweh's immediate action (vv 23-26).

The psalmist begins by focusing on Yahweh's discriminatory holy war activities.[48] Yahweh clearly distinguished between the enemy and Israel, i.e., he defeated the nations

---

[47] See. A. Weiser, *The Psalms*, 355.

[48] On the "re-presentation" of history in the communal lament see C. Westermann, "The 'Re-presentation' of History in the Psalms," *Praise and Lament*, 215-228.

but granted victory to his own people (v 2). The only response Israel made at that time was one of complete faith — military might was not needed (v 3). In verses 4-8 the psalmist continues this holy war motif. Israel's victories were due to Yahweh's exploits, a fact which Israel observed through a liturgy of praise (v 8).[49] However, in verses 9-16 the psalmist adopts a radically new tone because of the radically new state of affairs (note the "yet" in verse 9). The charge levelled against Yahweh is that he is now practicing reverse discrimination. Whereas Yahweh previously confused the enemy (v 7), he now confuses his own people instead. The signs of Yahweh's dereliction of duty are all too glaring: the enemy's looting (v 10), the dispersion of the prisoners in foreign countries (v 11), the scorn and ridicule suffered by Israel (vv 13-14). What adds insult to injury is the fact that Yahweh has not even behaved like a good merchant. He did not receive anything resembling a reasonable price when he sold off his property (v 12). Israel has unfortunately become the parade example of divine impotence.

In verses 17-22 Israel protests that her punishment is in no way commensurate with her behavior.[50] She has abided by the terms of the covenant (v 17) and has stayed the course asked of her (v 18). Nonetheless jackals make their dwellings in the ruins of the gutted cities (v 19). Surely this God must be aware of what is happening since nothing is hidden from him (vv 20-21). The damnable reality is that Israel suffers this excruciating dilemma because of Yahweh (v 22). "It is not the suffering in itself which in the first place causes such anxiety to the people's faith and makes it a real temptation

---

[49] On this aspect of lament R. J. Clifford ("Psalm 89: A Lament over the Davidic Ruler's Continued Failure," *Harvard Theological Review* 73 [1980] 39-40) observes: ". . . the psalmist complains that the people today have the same trusting attitude as did the ancestral generation of the conquest era, yet they are being defeated in battle. One therefore brings before God the original conquest whose power is still thought to be effective."

[50] See B. W. Anderson, "Sin and the Powers of Chaos," *Sin, Salvation, and the Spirit* (ed. D. Durken; Collegeville, Minnesota: The Liturgical Press, 1979) 76.

for them, but the fact that in their case it cannot be understood as a punishment."[51]

In verses 23-26 Israel takes the only course of action left.
It is the bold demand that this lethargic God wake up and
survey the situation (v 23). It is the audacious request that
Yahweh become conspicuous by his presence, not his
absence (v 24). Here the psalmist contrasts two positions: (a)
Israel's grovelling posture on the ground (v 25); and (b)
Yahweh's rising up as in the old days when he led her armies
to victory (see Num 10:35). Ths psalm concludes on the only
theological premise left to Israel, viz., Yahweh's covenant
fidelity (v 26: "steadfast love"). Though the devastation is
enormous and the pain all too acute, still hope for the
community resides, not in policies, plans, or programs, but
in a person. Yahweh must research his faithful actions of the
past so that he will be consistent in the present.

As a community at prayer, we must not hesitate to use the
bold language of this psalm. In the face of the threat of
nuclear warfare we must stir the Mighty Warrior to action.
In view of severe food shortages in various countries we
must incite Mother Yahweh to feed her family. In the light
of ongoing conflict in Latin America and the Near East we
must move the King to effect peace in his domain. It is
covenant which gives us the right to make such demands.
Not to employ such bold language at prayer is to deny our
status as a covenant community. We must not allow our
God to sleep any longer! Disorientation is never desirable
for its own sake.

Covenant is also calculated to make us reject our own
lethargy in the midst of the evils that plague fellow humans.
Community prayer is the moment to rise to the occasion and
have our God act through us. Community prayer is
designed to empower us to work for the present liberation of
fellow humans, not to sedate us to ponder our past benefac-
tions. As E. Wiesel has the Master tell Michael, "God is

[51] A. Weiser, *The Psalms*, 358.

imprisoned. Man must free him. That is the best-guarded secret since the Creation."[52] Our God will be freed to act to the extent that we remove his shackles. In community prayer we learn —painfully no doubt — that human presence can overcome divine absence. Ours is a God who not only trusts us but also needs us. At prayer we are urged not to abdicate the throne but to take our rightful place as kings and queens who hear the cries of the poor and then act. Community prayer is intended to teach us that fellow humans also have the right to impose on our sense of covenant loyalty so that the exodus from disorientation may begin.

Psalm 58[53]

> Do you indeed decree what is right, you gods?
> Do you judge the sons of men uprightly?
> [2]Nay, in your hearts you devise wrongs;
>> your hands deal out violence on earth.
> [3]The wicked go astray from the womb,
>> they err from their birth, speaking lies.
> [4]They have venom like the venom of a serpent,
>> like the deaf adder that stops its ear,
> [5]so that it does not hear the voice of charmers
>> or of the cunning enchanter.
>
> [6]O God, break the teeth in their mouths;
>> tear out the fangs of the young lions, O LORD!
> [7]Let them vanish like water that runs away;
>> like grass let them be trodden down and wither.
> [8]Let them be like the snail which dissolves into slime,
>> like the untimely birth that never sees the sun.
> [9]Sooner than your pots can feel the heat of thorns,
>> whether green or ablaze, may he sweep them away!
> [10]The righteous will rejoice when he sees the vengeance;

---

[52] E. Wiesel, *The Town Beyond the Wall*, 15.

[53] See A. Weiser, *The Psalms*, 429-432;   H. -J. Kraus, *Psalmen*, 415-419; H. H. Guthrie, *Israel's Sacred Songs*, 129-131.

he will bathe his feet in the blood of the wicked.
[11]Men will say, "Surely there is a reward for the righteous;
surely there is a God who judges on earth."

Regarding the original scene of this psalm K. Seybold has plausibly suggested that it is the divine tribunal of the Canaanite pantheon where the chief god El charges the other deities (v 1: "gods") with unjust judgments on earth. With regard to the theme it is the typical wisdom tradition of the establishment of a just order of things on earth.[54] In its Israelite form this psalm is a communal lament in which the petitioner places himself among the wronged. It thus becomes a prophetic denunciation with a petition for the punishment of the wrongdoers. Alonso Schökel divides the poem in this way: (a) appeal (v 1); (b) denunciation of the crime (vv 2-5); (c) petition for punishment (vv 6-9); (d) conclusion (vv 10-11).[55]

In denouncing the crime the poet proceeds in a general way, i. e., he does not offer a concrete report of specific crimes. Similarly the guilty form a group — they are not singled out as individuals. This suggests the danger whereby the powerful prefer to remain anonymous as they perpetrate their crimes. As Alonso Schökel also notes, the serpent plays a key role in the poetic development of the theme. The psalmist so portrays the serpent that it expresses the very manifestation of evil. Hence the psalm deals with evil as

[54]K. Seybold, "Psalm lviii. Ein Lösungsversuch." *VT* 30 (1980) 53-66. For a study of the root *šp̄* in the sense of saving the world from the oppression of the unjust see J. P. Miranda, *Marx and the Bible*, 111-137.

[55] L. Alonso Schökel, *Treinta Salmos*, 238.

[56] Ibid., 241. B. W. Anderson ("Sin and the Powers of Chaos," 81) offers this assessment of the serpent's role in Genesis 3: "In summary, Israel's historical experiences led to a profound apprehension of the power of evil which called for a correspondingly deep understanding of God's saving power. In the final analysis, the issue is not simply 'sin' and deserved punishment but the disturbance brought about by evil that infects human society and corrupts the course of human history. To return to the story of the Garden of Eden, the serpent that deceives is not just a beast of the field but, in a larger perspective, the mythical representation of the uncanny powers of chaos that the Divine Warrior must overcome in order to establish his kingdom."

such, not a particular instance of some concrete act of injustice.

In verses 6-9 the psalmist appeals to God's justice in maintaining order in the world. Consequently he utters curses whose fulfillment, viz., the utter destruction of the evildoers, will restore the imbalance. Some translate verse 7b differently, e.g., "If the enemy shoots arrows let their flight not be true."[57] Verse 9 is also difficult. Another translation is: "Unexpectedly, like a thorn-bush, or like thistles, let the whirlwind carry them away."[58] When Yahweh acts upon these petitions, the righteous person will rejoice as he bathes his feet in the blood of the perpetrators (v 10). God's redress will bear eloquent witness to his sense of justice (v 11).

In community prayer we must acknowledge the disorientation of injustice. The perversion of justice in whatever form contributes to the breakdown of equilibrium and harmony. In view of the violence inflicted by the powerful we must adopt the passionate language of Psalm 58. At prayer our task is not to foment violent action but to urge our God to restore justice to our world. As Alonso Schökel observes,[59] the thirst for justice is the thirst for the just God.

If our communal prayer is not to be a petition for the reign of justice only in heaven, then our prayer must help to establish that reign here on earth. Such prayer is the setting for posing these questions: who are those who practice injustice? where is the modern serpent? how does it operate? Our communal prayer must result in the conviction that whenever people experience injustice and violence (and hence disorientation) we all experience injustice and violence (and hence disorientation). Such prayer, if it is to

---

[57] B. Zerr, *The Psalms: A New Translation* (New York: Paulist, 1979) 124. M. Dahood (*Psalms 51-100*, 56) translates: "may he shoot his arrows like the emaciated."

[58] New American Bible. Unlike the RSV (see M. Dahood's remarks in *Psalms 51-100*, 62-63) the New American Bible duly notes that the Hebrew text is obscure.

[59] L. Alonso Schökel, *Treinta Salmos*, 242.

promote the move to reorientation, must insist more on our obligations than on our rights. Prayer is that disturbing encounter when we push aside the question "what can you do for us?" to dwell on "what must we do for you?" To pray to this covenant God is to commit our communities to the needs of all his children. Justice is simply the acknowledgement that we no longer regard disorientation as the ordinary state of our brothers and sisters. The abuse of power in our church and in our society at large can never be standard business procedure.

Psalm 85[60]

> Lord, thou wast favorable to thy land;
>   thou didst restore the fortunes of Jacob.
> [2]Thou didst forgive the iniquity of thy people;
>   thou didst pardon all their sin.
>
>   *Selah*
> [3]Thou didst withdraw all thy wrath;
>   thou didst turn from thy hot anger.
> [4]Restore us again, O God of our salvation,
>   and put away thy indignation toward us!
> [5]Wilt thou be angry with us for ever?
>   Wilt thou prolong thy anger to all generations?
> [6]Wilt thou not revive us again,
>   that thy people may rejoice in thee?
> [7]Show us thy steadfast love, O LORD,
>   and grant us thy salvation.
>
> [8]Let me hear what God the LORD will speak,
>   for he will speak peace to his people,
>   to his saints, to those who turn to him in their hearts.
> [9]Surely his salvation is at hand for those who fear him,
>   that glory may dwell in our land.
>
> [10]Steadfast love and faithfulness will meet;
>   righteousness and peace will kiss each other.

[60]See A. Weiser, *The Psalms*, 570-575; H.-J. Kraus, *Psalmen*, 570-575.

[11]Faithfulness will spring up from the ground,
  and righteousness will look down from the sky.
[12]Yea, the LORD will give what is good,
  and our land will yield its increase.
[13]Righteousness will go before him,
  and make his footsteps a way.

As a lament, this psalm lacks the penetrating wrath of Psalm 74 and the despondent note of Psalm 44. While it focuses on Israel's problem, it accentuates the type of response expected of God's people. It is a meditation on the meaning of peace and the manner of acquiring it. Although it perhaps originally depicted the exile, within the Psalter it takes on wider meaning by suggesting the program of peace in other situations of dire need. It may be divided as follows: (a) previous experience of grace (vv 1-3); (b) request for renewal and return from exile (vv 4-7); (c) oracle of salvation (vv 8-9); (d) covenant renewal (vv 10-13).

The first section (vv 1-3) offers a solid reason for Israel's hope, viz., Yahweh has acted favorably in the past. Not surprisingly the land motif appears (v 1) since peace obviously has something to do with the land. In previous times of upheaval and disruption Yahweh placed greater emphasis on grace than on his burning anger (v 3). This recollection now prompts the people's plea: restoration (v 4), overcoming divine wrath (v 5), renewal as the setting for praise (v 6), and the positive demonstration of covenant concern (v 7). At this point the psalmist puts aside any recital of Yahweh's past salvific deeds. He simply pronounces a prophetic oracle assuring peace because the God of Israel is ever with his people (vv 8-9). It is significant, however, that God's presence hinges on the people's response. The Hebrew text concluding verse 8 states that the speaking of peace is bound up with the people's fidelity, i.e., provided they do not return to their foolish ways. As D. J. McCarthy observed, God's gift and human response create a problem. "The problem is combining loving gift and earned reward. The danger is in choosing the second . . . we are more comfortable with reliance on ourselves, with the feeling that we have done all we can . . ."[61]

In the last section the land theme of verse 1 is taken up again. Verse 12 can create the impression that peace consists only in the absence of violence and the presence of material prosperity. However, the covenant vocabulary of this conclusion assures us that our impression is inadequate. Faithfulness (vv 10,11) implies total dedication.[62] Righteousness (vv 10,11) means proper order and justice and hence peace. This final section "turns to a peace which is harmony, first of all between man and God. Love and faithfulness are to meet; that is, we are to give ourselves to him who is overwhelming love and fidelity . . ."[63]

At community prayer we must dwell on God's call and our response. In order to achieve peace in the aftermath of disorientation we must express our willingness to accept this God and reject all those false idols which detract from covenant union. To overcome disorientation as a community, we must open ourselves to the point of being totally grounded in this Yahweh. Community prayer means, therefore, the dismantling of our anxieties, doubts, and despair. Reorientation is the embrace of realism: the acceptance of the covenant God and his demands. Life based on false goals and preoccupations can only result in greater alienation. Community prayer basically means renewing the terms of our community life: life with this God and his people.

---

[61] D. J. McCarthy, "Psalm 85 and the Meaning of Peace," *The Way* 22 (1982) 6.

[62] J. S. Kselman ("A Note on Psalm 85:9-10," *CBQ* 46 [1984] 26) offers the following translation and paraphrase of verses 8-9: "Let me declare what El decrees, what Yahweh says — for he promises peace (*šlwm*) to the devoted ones of his people, to the one who dwells in security. Surely, near is his salvation to those who fear him; near is his glory to him who dwells in the land . . . God promises peace and proclaims the proximity of his glorious salvation to the people bound to him in covenant, who fear him and dwell in the land in security."

[63] D. J. McCarthy, "Psalm 85," 8. On Hosea's vivid picture of covenant disruption and covenant restoration in chapter 2 see W. Brueggemann, *Tradition for Crisis: A Study in Hosea* (Atlanta: John Knox, 1968) 110-119.

Community prayer is the time for pronouncing oracles. In and through prayer our God charges us as a community to proclaim the message of peace to our world. This implies alerting our people to the powers of oppression and empowering them to dare to hope again. This involves a theology of revelation. It is the unmasking of false values which tend to usurp the place of our God (power, violence, unbridled ambition, etc.). It is the presentation of true values which announce the abiding presence of our God (justice, mercy, love, etc.).[64] In this way our world will yearn to be healed and so cope with disorientation. It will also resist clutching an egocentric past and thus move on to reorientation. Prayer is the setting in motion of the plan of peace: harmony between God and humans, harmony between fellow humans, harmony between humans and the world of nature. Prayer assures us that the vision is no utopia.

Psalm 89[65]

> I will sing of thy steadfast love,
>   O LORD, for ever;
> with my mouth I will proclaim thy
>   faithfulness to all generations.
> [2]For thy steadfast love was established for ever,
>   thy faithfulness is firm as the heavens.
> [3]Thou hast said, "I have made a covenant with my chosen
>   one,

[64]On the prophetic role of energizing see W. Brueggemann, *The Prophetic Experience*, 62-79.

[65]See A. Weiser, *The Psalms*, 587-594; H. -J. Kraus, *Psalmen,* 612-626; G. W. Ahlström, *Psalm 89: Eine Liturgie aus dem Ritual des leidenden Königs* (Lund: Gleerup, 1959); J. Hofbauer, "Ps. LXXXVIII (LXXXIX) — Sein Aufbau, sein Herkunft und seine Stellung in der Theologie des Alten Testaments," *Sacra Pagina* (ed. J. Coppens et al.; Gembloux: Duculot, 1959), 1. 504-510; J. M. Ward, "The Literary Form and Liturgical Background of Psalm LXXXIX," *VT* 11 (1961) 320-339; N. Sarna, "Psalm 89: A Study in Inner Biblical Exegesis," *Biblical and Other Studies* (ed. A. Altman; Cambridge: Harvard University, 1963) 29-46; E. Lipiński, *Le poème royal de Psaume LXXXIX 1-5.20-38* (Cahiers de la Revue biblique 6; Paris: Gabalda, 1967); F. M. Cross, *Canaanite Myth and Hebrew Epic*, 160-162, 257-261; S. Terrien, *The Elusive Presence*, 298-304.

I have sworn to David my servant:
4"I will establish your descendants for ever,
    and build your throne for all generations.'"
                                                Selah
5Let the heavens praise thy wonders, O LORD,
    thy faithfulness in the assembly of the holy ones!
6For who in the skies can be compared to the LORD?
    Who among the heavenly beings is like the LORD,
7a God feared in the council of the holy ones,
    great and terrible above all that are round about him?
8O LORD God of hosts,
    who is mighty as thou art, O LORD,
    with thy faithfulness round about thee?
9Thou dost rule the raging of the sea;
    when its waves rise, thou stillest them.
10Thou didst crush Rahab like a carcass,
    thou didst scatter thy enemies with thy mighty arm.
11The heavens are thine, the earth also is thine;
    the world and all that is in it,
    thou hast founded them.
12The north and the south, thou hast created them;
    Tabor and Hermon joyously praise thy name.
13Thou hast a mighty arm;
    strong is thy hand, high thy right hand.
14Righteousness and justice are the foundation of thy
throne;
    steadfast love and faithfulness go before thee.

15Blessed are the people who know the festal shout,
    who walk, O LORD, in the light of thy countenance,
16who exult in thy name all the day,
    and extol thy righteousness.
17For thou art the glory of their strength;
    by thy favor our horn is exalted.
18For our shield belongs to the LORD,
    our king to the Holy One of Israel.

19Of old thou didst speak in a vision

to thy faithful one, and say:
"I have set the crown upon one who is mighty,
I have exalted one chosen from the people.
[20]I have found David, my servant;
with my holy oil I have anointed him;
[21]so that my hand shall ever abide with him,
my arm also shall strengthen him.
[22]The enemy shall not outwit him,
the wicked shall not humble him.
[23]I will crush his foes before him
and strike down those who hate him.
[24]My faithfulness and my steadfast love shall be with him,
and in my name shall his horn be exalted.
[25]I will set his hand on the sea and his right hand on the
rivers.
[26]"He shall cry to me, 'Thou art my Father,
my God, and the Rock of my salvation.'
[27]And I will make him the first-born,
the highest of the kings of the earth.
[28]My steadfast love I will keep for him for ever,
and my covenant will stand firm for him.
[29]I will establish his line for ever
and his throne as the days of the heavens.
[30]"If his children forsake my law
and do not walk according to my ordinances,
[31]if they violate my statutes
and do not keep my commandments,
[32]then I will punish their transgression with the rod
and their iniquity with scourges;
[33]but I will not remove from him my steadfast love,
or be false to my faithfulness.
[34]I will not violate my covenant,
or alter the word that went forth from my lips.
[35]Once for all I have sworn by my holiness;
I will not lie to David.
[36]His line shall endure for ever,
his throne as long as the sun before me.

³⁷Like the moon it shall be established for ever;
    it shall stand firm while the skies endure."

                                                  Selah

³⁸But now thou hast cast off and rejected,
    thou art full of wrath against thy anointed.
³⁹Thou hast renounced the covenant with thy servant;
    thou hast defiled his crown in the dust.
⁴⁰Thou hast breached all his walls;
    thou hast laid his strongholds in ruins.
⁴¹All that pass by despoil him;
    he has become the scorn of his neighbors.

⁴²Thou hast exalted the right hand of his foes;
    thou hast made all his enemies rejoice.
⁴³Yea, thou hast turned back the edge of his sword,
    and thou hast not made him stand in battle.
⁴⁴Thou hast removed the scepter from his hand,
    and cast his throne to the ground.
⁴⁵Thou hast cut short the days of his youth;
    thou hast covered him with shame.

                                                  Selah

⁴⁶How long, O LORD? Wilt thou hide thyself for ever?
    How long will thy wrath burn like fire?
⁴⁷Remember, O Lord, what the measure of life is,
    for what vanity thou hast created
    all the sons of men!
⁴⁸What man can live and never see death?
    Who can deliver his soul from the power of Sheol?

                                                  Selah

⁴⁹Lord, where is thy steadfast love of old,
    which by thy faithfulness thou didst swear to David?
⁵⁰Remember, O Lord, how thy servant is scorned;
    how I bear in my bosom the insults of the peoples,
⁵¹with which thy enemies taunt, O LORD,
    with which they mock the footsteps of thy anointed.

⁵²Blessed be the LORD for ever!
    Amen and Amen.

The composition of the psalm poses problems. There seem to be three distinct parts: (a) cosmic hymn (vv 1-18); (b) divine oracle (vv 19-37); (c) lament (vv 38-51). (Verse 52 is the conclusion of Book Three of the Psalter). Many think that the hymn was added to the lament by interposing the divine oracle. However, R. J. Clifford has plausibly argued that the entire psalm was written as a coherent communal lament.[66] Verses 1-37 describe one event, viz., the acclamation of Yahweh's establishment of the world/Israel and the Davidic dynasty. In turn, the lament (vv 38-51) occasioned by the king's powerlessness appears to negate Yahweh's victory. (This powerlessness is depicted in general terms and hence is applicable to a variety of political defeats.) The psalm may be divided as follows: (a) Yahweh's victory: (i) hymnic introduction (vv 1-4); (ii) acclamation of Yahweh's creation of the world/Israel (vv 5-18); (iii) promise to David and his descendants as part of the celebration of Yahweh's creation of the world/Israel (vv 19-37); (b) lament because of the king's powerlessness (vv 38-51).

In the hymnic introduction the psalmist emphasizes Yahweh's covenant commitment (v 2: "steadfast love," "faithfulness"). It is these qualities which provide solidity for the world. According to verse 14 these qualities are linked to the King's cosmic activities. Significantly God's choice of David is eternal like the order established in creation (vv 28-29). Moreover, the heavenly bodies reflect Yahweh's covenant qualities which undergird the divine promise to the Davidic dynasty. The Davidic king who represents Yahweh on earth enjoys power that is directly proportionate to Yahweh's power.[67] However, the present powerlessness of the king threatens to undermine heaven's eternal order. The psalmist registers the great danger by asking in verse 49: "Lord, where is thy steadfast love of old, which by thy faithfulness

[66] R. J. Clifford, "Psalm 89," 36.

[67] See J. -B. Dumortier, "Un rituel d'intronisation: Le Ps LXXXIX:2-38," *VT* 22 (1972) 187.

thou didst swear to David?" Hence the predicament experienced by the community calls into question Yahweh's pledged word and with it the equilibrium of the cosmos. The king's disorientation is the people's disorientation which in the end is also Yahweh's disorientation.

The psalmist skillfully links Yahweh's cosmic achievements to the promised achievements of his earthly representative.[68] Just as Yahweh's hand defeated the powers of chaos and delivered Israel (v 13), that same hand will abide to win victories for the king (v 21). Just as Yahweh overcame cosmic enemies (vv 9-10), his viceroy will overcome earthly enemies (vv 22-23). Just as covenant commitment and faithfulness characterize the divine throne (v 14), they will also support the human throne (v 24a). As Clifford remarks, "... the regent of Yahweh, at least *in potentia*, is the most powerful king on earth."[69]

The pathos of the lament reveals itself in the first two words of verse 39: "but now." The king's crown and scepter now lie in the dust (vv 39,44). The walls have been breached and the strongholds gutted (v 40). The king is now the object of scorn (v 41), not adulation. The enemy's hand (v 42) has been exalted, not the king's (v 21). The enemy's sword (v 43) has been victorious in battle, not the king's (see verses 22-23). Yet even in view of military disaster or failure in international politics Israel clings tenaciously to her faith. She recalls Yahweh's pledged word in creation and, with that, in the commission to David. With that recollection she holds Yahweh to his word. After all, Israel's anointed king is also Yahweh's anointed king (v 51).

At prayer we are not to block out the tragic news of ongoing war and further intrigue in international politics in order to resort to that dream world where the big powers are absent and bigger and better weapons of destruction are screened out. At community prayer we cannot evade this

---

[68] See L. Vosberg, *Studien zum Reden vom Schöpfer in den Psalmen* (Munich: Kaiser, 1975) 31-35.

[69] R. J. Clifford, "Psalm 89," 45.

state of disorientation because this is our world and we have no other. The distressing reports from the distant corners of the globe must become the substance of our common prayer. Ours is a God who once established harmony in his creation and who continues to reestablish that harmony despite human violence and viciousness. In the setting of prayer we dare not forget that our God takes a vested interest in his creation simply because he pledged his word. In the less than polite language of the communal lament we are to remind this God of his pledged word and press him to assess the situation and act quickly. Like Israel, we must observe the discrepancy between promise and reality.

At communal prayer we must also review our position as our God's viceroys. This God has commissioned us to be the sustaining force in his creation, to be the agents of order, not disorder. In the trek from disorientation to reorientation we must recall that we are our God's privileged kings and queens who must respond to human powerlessness. To be instruments of harmony in creation means to realize that we can and do make a difference. We have pledged our word in so many different settings, from the saluting of our flag to the saluting of our neighbor. The pain and frustration of countless humans appeal to our sense of covenant commitment and loyalty, precisely as a community. Ironically the great cosmic God chooses us to defeat the powers of chaos. Famine, discrimination, threat of nuclear warfare, and political oppression are but a few of the disruptive manifestations of that chaos. To be involved in communal prayer is to be empowered and commissioned to speak out and act. Prayer in that sense is our most powerful political weapon.

Psalm 90[70]

> Lord, thou hast been our dwelling place in all generations.
> [2]Before the mountains were brought forth,

[70]See A. Weiser, *The Psalms*, 594-603; H. - J. Kraus, *Psalmen*, 627-633.

or ever thou hadst formed the earth and the world,
from everlasting to everlasting thou art God.
³Thou turnest man back to the dust,
and sayest, "Turn back, O children of men!
⁴For a thousand years in thy sight
are but as yesterday when it is past,
or as a watch in the night.

⁵Thou dost sweep men away; they are like a dream,
like grass which is renewed in the morning:
⁶in the morning it flourishes and is renewed;
in the evening it fades and withers.
⁷For we are consumed by thy anger;
by thy wrath we are overwhelmed.
⁸Thou hast set our iniquities before thee,
our secret sins in the light of thy countenance.

⁹For all our days pass away under thy wrath,
our years come to an end like a sigh.
¹⁰The years of our life are threescore and ten,
or even by reason of strength fourscore;
yet their span is but toil and trouble;
they are soon gone, and we fly away.

¹¹Who considers the power of thy anger.
and thy wrath according to the fear of thee?
¹²So teach us to number our days
that we may get a heart of wisdom.
¹³Return, O LORD! How long?
Have pity on thy servants!
¹⁴Satisfy us in the morning with thy steadfast love,
that we may rejoice and be glad all our days.
¹⁵Make us glad as many days as thou hast afflicted us,
and as many years as we have seen evil.
¹⁶Let thy work be manifest to thy servants,
and thy glorious power to their children.
¹⁷Let the favor of the Lord our God be upon us,
and establish thou the work of our hands upon us,
yea, the work of our hands establish thou it.

This communal lament which is pronounced by an individual does not provide any specific background. Alonso Schokel describes it as a meditation on human life in the light of God which ends in petition.[71] Weiser suggests much the same: "Here a man with the mature experience of old age looks back upon human life and against the background of the eternal being of God apprehends its nature and its ultimate coherence."[72] The poem may be divided as follows: (a) the contrast between human duration and divine eternity (vv 1-6); (b) the consciousness of divine wrath because of human sinfulness (vv 7-11); (c) petitions for coping in life (vv 12-17).[73] Thus up to verse 11 there is a descent from the sadness of mortality to the tragedy of sin and divine wrath. However, with verse 12 there is an ascent to the point of both accepting and coping.

In the first section the psalmist begins with a recollection of God's help and assistance in the past which is at the same time an appeal for help and assistance in the present. The poet's choice of "refuge" (v 1) (rather than RSV's "dwelling place") immediately conjures up the image of something stable. Against the background of God's eternity (v 2) the human condition is anything but stable. Borrowing from the traditions of Genesis 2-3, the psalmist insists on the frailty of human nature (v 3). Time, moreover, is really on God's side: a thousand years is a mere nothing. While God is eternal, humans experience vitality only to see it elude them in a moment (vv 5-6).

Human sinfulness makes human life all the more difficult. Israel's God is not an impersonal force or energy. Yahweh is truly a person who is provoked to anger by Israel's sins (vv 7,9,11).[74] Humans reject life because they reject the author

---

[71] L. Alonso Schökel, *Treinta Salmos*, 313.

[72] A. Weiser, *The Psalms*, 595.

[73] For further structural studies of Psalm 900 see S. Schreiner, "Erwägungen zur Struktur des 90. Psalms," *Biblica* 59 (1978) 80-90; P. Auffret, "Essai sur la structure littéraire du Psaume 90," *Biblica* 61 (1980) 262-276.

[74] See A. J. Heschel, *The Prophets* (New York: Harper & Row, 1962) 279-306.

of life by their sins. Even their hidden sins cannot evade the scrutiny of this totally involved deity. Even if they should live to be seventy or eighty (an exaggeration given the relatively short age spans of the time), they experience only toil and trouble (v 10).

Finally in verse 12 a dire reflection gives way to petition. In commenting on a "heart of wisdom" G. von Rad wrote: "Wisdom in the Old Testament is something extremely sober. It is the knowledge of life and the art of living, the adaptation to all realities, to which belong also the realities of man's relationship to God."[75] In seeking to live, Israel engages the Living One. His covenant presence (v 14) makes life not only tolerable but also enjoyable. Israel next prays that this God will compensate them in proportion to the evil sustained (v 15). In verse 16 the community seeks to reawaken its sense of God's past activity for the needs of the present. Recalling such history offers the means to cope. Finally Israel asks God's blessing on her work (v 17). According to Alonso Schökel's observation human work, affirmed and directed by God, is proof of his goodness, shares in his efficacy and fecundity, and gives meaning and fullness to life.[76]

At prayer the community is often the doubting community, the sinful community. Disorientation is not infrequently the result of an all too limited wisdom. We tend to see life as the accumulation of goods, the heaping up of distinctions, and the solidity of our own ego. Like the couple in the garden, we make ourselves the norm of conduct and reject that wisdom which resides in genuine living.[77] The move from disorientation to reorientation begins by acknowledg-

[75] G. von Rad, "Psalm 90," *God at Work in Israel*, 216-217.

[76] L. Alonso Schökel, *Treinta Salmos*, 323.

[77] On the wisdom dimension of the Garden of Eden account see G. E. Mendenhall, "The Shady Side of Wisdom: The Date and Purpose of Genesis 3," *A Light Unto my Path: Old Testament Studies in Honor of Jacob M. Myers* (ed. H. N. Bream et al.; Gettysburg Theological Studies 4; Philadelphia: Temple University, 1974) 319-334.

ing that we must be caught up with this God, not a program of action. Community prayer must also bring us to realize that our sinfulness cannot defeat our God and indeed that it may be the point of departure for wise living. Because of covenant we can even demand that God's past activities on our behalf (v 16) be recognized as the precedent for help here and now. Community prayer is an exercise in recommitting ourselves to the belief that God, our community, and individuals have to interact as healthy covenant partners. Wisdom and hence the defeat of disorientation is our renewed enthusiasm to live, not exist, to celebrate, not tolerate.

Community prayer must also be operation outreach for those who doubt about God, the community, and especially themselves. To pray this communal lament is to share its conviction with such people. The work and glorious power of our God (v 16) must be the community's contribution to the despairing. Essentially our prayer must be to teach them wisdom for the delicate art of living. In the face of human doubts and human sinfulness we must nonetheless share a God who calls us to happiness, who offers us the gift of his covenant presence, and who interacts in our work. To crush disorientation is to strike a blow for healthy community life. Community prayer is a demanding enterprise.

New Testament

Mark 15:21-39

21And they compelled a passer-by, Simon of Cyrene, who was coming in from the country, the father of Alexander and Rufus, to carry his cross.22 And they brought him to the place called Golgotha (which means the place of a skull). 23And they offered him wine mingled with myrrh; but he did not take it. 24And they crucified him, and divided his garments among them, casting lots for them, to decide what each should take. [25]And it was the third hour, when they crucified him. [26]And the inscription of the charge against him read, "The King of the Jews." [27]And with him they crucified two robbers, one on his right and one on his left. [29]And those who passed by derided him, wagging their heads, and saying, "Aha! You who would destroy the temple and build it in three days, [30]save yourself, and come down from the cross!" [31]So also the chief priests mocked him to one another with the scribes, saying, "He saved others; he cannot save himself. [32]Let the Christ, the King of Israel, come down now from the cross, that we may see and believe." Those who were crucified with him also reviled him.

[33]And when the sixth hour had come, there was darkness over the whole land until the ninth hour." [34]And at the ninth hour Jesus cried with a loud voice, Eloi, Eloi, lama sabachthani?" which means, "My God, my God, why hast thou forsaken me?" And some of the bystanders hearing it said, "Behold, he is calling Elijah." [36]And one ran and, filling a sponge full of vinegar, put it on a reed and gave it to him to drink, saying "Wait, let us see whether Elijah will come to take him down." [37]And Jesus uttered a loud cry, and breathed his last. [38]And the curtain of the temple was torn in two, from top to bottom, [39]And when the centurion, who stood facing him, saw that he thus breathed his last, he said, "Truly this man was the Son of God!"

It is clear that Psalm 22 plays a central role in Mark's account of the suffering and death of Jesus.[78] The dividing of the garments in 15:24 calls to mind: "they divide my garments among them, and for my raiment they cast lots" (Ps 22:18). The jeering and mockery of the chief priests in

---

[78]See H. – J. Kraus, *Theologie der Psalmen*, 238-241.

15:31 reflect: "All who see me mock at me, they make mouths at me, they wag their heads; 'He committed his cause to the Lord; let him deliver him, let him rescue him, for he delights in him!'" (Ps 22:7-8). Jesus' cry of dereliction in 15:34 cites: "My God, my God, why hast thou forsaken me?" (Ps 22:1). Whether or not Jesus actually uttered this saying is a matter of dispute. For some[79] the cry from the cross is an authentic word of Jesus. For others[80] the evidence for a genuine word of Jesus is insufficient. In any event what is clear is Mark's understanding of the mystery of the cross.[81]

According to Mark Jesus comes to execute the Father's plan. He is the Son of Man who chooses to give his life as "a ransom for many" (Mk 10:45). Such a Jesus is a suffering Son of Man whose relationship to the Father hinges on obedience. Suffering and obedience were traditional in Israel's psalms of lament. For Mark Jesus epitomizes the righteous sufferer in these psalms.[82] However, Mark does not end his account with the suffering. The Father trans-

---

[79]See H. D. Lange, "The Relationship Between Psalm 22 and the Passion Narrative," *CTM* 43 (1972) 610-621. L. R. Fisher ("Betrayed by Friends — An Expository Study of Psalm 22," *Int* 18 [1964] 20-38) holds that Jesus also used Psalm 22 as his lament. However, he maintains that it is not God who forsakes him, but rather his friends.

[80]See J. H. Reumann, "Psalm 22 at the Cross — Lament and Thanksgiving for Jesus Christ," *Int* 28 (1974) 39-58. W. Brueggemann (*The Land*, 182-183) links Psalm 22 to the passion by way of underlining the movement from landlessness to landedness.

[81]See A. Stock, *Call to Discipleship*, 191-202.

[82]Against the background of overcoming power and violence E. Haag ("Die Botschaft vom Gottesknecht — Ein Weg zur Überwindung der Gewalt," *Gewalt und Gewaltlosigkeit im Alten Testament*, 159-213) examines the message of the Servant in Second Isaiah's Suffering Servant songs. The author takes the mediatorial role of the original individual and applies it to the true Israel that has been saved from the Babylonian exile. This servant confronts a world of violent deeds and lies. It is his task to bring judgment to this world. However, he does not accomplish this as Israel earlier accomplished it, viz., by the violence of warfare. When this powerful world attacks him, he does not take up the challenge by striking back. Rather, he vicariously assumes the punishment which would otherwise overtake the guilty. He rejects all violence and yet is the victim of violence. In this way, however, he helps to make possible that new form of salvation which stems from God but no longer relies on violence.

forms the suffering into victory.[83] "No matter which view commends itself, use of Psalm 22 through the pre-Christian centuries and critical analysis of our Gospels working back from them to Jesus meet in a picture of the cross as lament in suffering and thanksgiving for what God then did. To that extent the intent of the psalm came to supreme expression in Jesus."[84]

Disorientation is all too patent in Jesus' experience of pain and frustration. The cry of dereliction is the prayer of lament that the Father now make Jesus' problem his problem. On the other hand, the reality of the cross is that Jesus must make the Father's problem his problem, viz., the redemption by means of suffering and death. Thus Jesus is bidden to let go, to relinquish the old securities, to accept the paradox of Calvary. Reorientation is the embrace of the Father at Easter. The resurrection is the clearest sign that Jesus is on a new level of being.

Second Corinthians 11:30-12:10

> [30]If I must boast, I will boast of the things that show my weakness. [31]The God and Father of the Lord Jesus, he who is blessed for ever, knows that I do not lie. [32]At Damascus, the governor under King Aretas guarded the city of Damascus in order to seize me, [33]but I was let down in a basket through a window in the wall, and escaped his hands.
>
> 12 I must boast; there is nothing to be gained by it, but I will go on to visions and revelations of the Lord. [2]I know a man in Christ who fourteen years ago was caught up to the third heaven — whether in the body or out of the body I do not know, God knows. [3]And I know that this man was caught up into Paradise — whether in the body or

---

[83] H. Gese ("Psalm 22 und das Neue Testament," *Zeitschrift für Theologie und Kirche* 65 [1968] 1-22 — summarized as "Psalm 22 and the New Testament, *Theology Digest* 18 [1970] 237-243) sees the thanksgiving liturgy of Psalm 22 realized in the celebration of the Lord's Supper.

[84] J. H. Reumann, "Psalm 22 at the Cross," 58.

out of the body I do not know, God knows — ⁴and he heard things that cannot be told, which man may not utter. ⁵On behalf of this man I will boast, but on my own behalf I will not boast, except of my weaknesses. ⁶Though if I wish to boast, I shall not be a fool, for I shall be speaking the truth. But I refrain from it, so that no one may think more of me than he sees in me or hears from me.

⁷And to keep me from being too elated by the abundance of revelations, a thorn was given me in the flesh, a messenger of Satan, to harass me, to keep me from being too elated. ⁸Three times I besought the Lord about this, that it should leave me; ⁹but he said to me, "My grace is sufficient for you, for my power is made perfect in weakness." I will all the more gladly boast of my weaknesses, that the power of Christ may rest upon me.

¹⁰For the sake of Christ, then, I am content with weaknesses, insults, hardships, persecutions, and calamities; for when I am weak, then I am strong.

In Second Corinthians 11-12 Paul takes up his manner of ministry. Although the text is a letter and not a lament, it nevertheless suggests the thrust of lament in coping with weakness, a stance not unlike that in Mark's passion account.

In replying to his opponents, Paul states that he too can boast about his Jewish background (11:22), his labors (11:23-29), and his visions (12:1-4). However, Paul prefers a different approach, viz., boasting about his weaknesses.[85] "If I must boast, I will boast of the things that show my weakness" (11:30). He takes the same stance in 12:5. For

---

[85]See T. Y. Mullins, "Paul's Thorn in the Flesh," *JBL* 76 (1957) 299-303; G. O'Collins, "Power Made Perfect in Weakness (2 Cor 12:9-10)," *CBQ* 33 (1971) 528-537; D. M. Stanley, *Boasting in the Lord: The Phenomenon of Prayer in Saint Paul* (New York: Paulist, 1973) 52-60; "Power and Weakness — Dialectic of Healing within the Healing Community," *The Way* 16 (1976) 176-188; M. L. Barré, "Paul as 'Eschatologic Person' — A New Look at 2 Cor 11:29," *CBQ* 37 (1975) 509-514; "Qumran and the 'Weakness' of Paul," *CBQ* 42 (1980) 216-227.

Paul weakness is not merely a declaration about the present state of affairs. Rather, weakness has an intrinsic power to extricate a person from the incrustations of ego and so to move one to look beyond oneself to Christ. Far from disparaging his ministry, weakness becomes the symbol of apostolic authority and legitimation.[86] "For the sake of Christ, then, I am content with weaknesses, . . . ; for when I am weak, then I am strong" (12:10). Paul thus exemplifies the disorientation-reorientation process. By his willingness to let go, to relinquish the self-oriented patterns of ministry, he is able to embrace Christ and the experience of the transformation power of the resurrection.

Paul's manner of thinking and acting flies in the face of our pragmatic business procedures. In applying for jobs, we do not notify the prospective employer about our weaknesses and failures. We choose to dwell on our strengths and successes in the hope that they will win the position for us. It is so difficult for us to accept Paul's theology, viz., that in weakness power reaches perfection (see 12:10). Too often we have conceived of our God as the Celestial Personnel Officer who peruses dossiers and makes final determinations as a result of them. At prayer Paul suggests that we focus on the weakness of the Crucified and thus derive strength for our mission. For Paul there is no detour around Calvary in the faith approach to overcoming disorientation. Paul was clearly in touch with his Old Testament prayer of lament.

Summary of the theology of the laments[87]

(1) The laments, both individual and communal, are a school of prayer. They demand that we meet life head-on

---

[86]See M. Neumann, "Ministry, Weakness, and Spirit in II Corinthians," *Clergy Review* 59 (1974) 647-660; H. J. M. Nouwen, "The Monk and the Cripple — Toward a Spirituality of Ministry," *America* 142 (March 15, 1980) 205-210.

[87]Other laments include the following: (a) individual: 4-7, 10, 13-14 (see 53), 17, 25-28, 35-36, 38, 51, 54-57, 59, 61, 63-64, 70-71, 86, 88, 102, 109, 120, 130, 140-143; (b) communal: 12, 74, 79-80, 83, 94, 123, 126, 129, 137.

and thereby eschew the role of faking and making-believe.

(2) We are bidden to let go of the securities of the past and see the precariousness of the present not simply as a crisis but as a faith opportunity. Hence the situation can mean growth, not demise.

(3) The laments are a study in human weakness. We are asked to look beyond ourselves to a generous God who creates us in the image of his Son, i.e., as weak humans.

(4) We are invited to see the weaknesses inherent in our ministry and make them the vehicle for God's presence. To cope with tragedy and pain is to announce that we do not travel by ourselves.

(5) The lament of Jesus (as well as the laments of Jeremiah) demands that we open ourselves up to the larger contours of our God's world of concern. We are forcefully reminded that covenant is a two-edged sword. By asking help in our world of frustration, we are implicitly committed to offering help in our God's world of frustration, viz., other people. To cry for help means to be willing to hear the community's cry for help.

7

To a God of Surprises
The Psalms of Declarative Praise

Surprise versus control

The rumor has been verified: most of us do not like to be surprised. To be surprised implies that we have surrendered at least some of our autonomy, i.e., an event has occurred over which we have exercised little or no control. To be surprised further suggests that other people are invading the sacred domain of our independence. As a result, we program ourselves to eliminate all vestiges of surprise. When a seeming surprise does occur, we offer the explanation that we had a remote hand in its making. Hence it is not really a surprise at all.

We prefer to operate on the basis of checks and balances, cause and effect, energy expended and results obtained. In our ledgers everything must balance out. Otherwise we run the risk of distorting our prefabricated harmony. Therefore, we choose to focus on the things that we produced or manufactured. We find it exceedingly difficult to dwell on things that did not come off our assembly line. We dare not appreciate sunsets or symphonies because we would thereby admit that we did not produce them. And yet they are there yearning to be enjoyed, not merely stored away in the indifferent memory bank of our computers.

If somehow we get to the point where we can be surprised by things, we remain on principle opposed to being surprised by humans. They are not calculated, we think, to demonstrate the creativity of the deity. Hence they dare not surprise us by their goodness. To offset this remote possibility, we reduce people to things, objects ready to provide us with instant pleasure, should the need arise. In our obsession we are precluded from asking these type of questions: in what way do these people reflect the Creator's image? How warm is their love and how great is their compassion? We do not want to be surprised because the truly human qualities of others will reveal the selfishness of our inhumanity.

We are victims suffering from the demise of celebration. We have lost the radical ability to party, to have a good time. Hand in hand with our loss of celebration goes our loss of the sense of mystery. We do not want to celebrate the attainments of others because we have already labelled them as unproductive. It is so painful to congratulate others because we choose not to break free from our ego-incarcerated world. To celebrate and congratulate would demand a new vision of reality.

At prayer we are challenged to believe in a God of surprises and indeed a God who surprises us through others. The breakthrough from disorientation to reorientation is in the nature of gift or grace. To pray to this God is to put aside our efforts at control. To pray to this God is to admit amazement and bewilderment which stem from Another and are not the total result of our human efforts. This God is a God of surprises who invites us to marvel at his manifold gifts. The move from disorientation to reorientation is by way of gift-giving.[1] And such gift-giving demands that we recover our sense of celebration. At prayer we must recapture for ourselves the truth that this is a God who likes parties because it is the nature of this God to give.

Thanksgivings or psalms of declarative praise

C. Westermann has consistently pointed out that the Hebrew verb "to thank" does not have the connotations that

---

[1] T. Merton (*Bread in the Wilderness*, 67-70, 122) speaks of reorientation as transformation whereby one becomes someone else.

we moderns associate with the granting of a request. In its biblical usage "to thank" is "to praise."[2] For Westermann, moreover, there is no separate psalm genre known as thanksgiving. Rather, there is one basic genre of praise in the psalms with two different aspects:

> "The difference between the two groups lies in the fact that the so-called hymn praises God for his actions and his being as a whole (descriptive praise), while the so-called song of thanks praises God for a specific deed, which the one who has been delivered recounts or reports in his song (declarative praise: ...).[3]

As noted earlier, Westermann's view has attracted dissenting voices. Leaving open Westermann's form-critical identification of psalms of praise, W. Brueggemann stresses the function of thanksgivings or psalms of declarative praise. For Brueggemann these psalms do not merely describe but actually assert the presence of newness.[4] For F. Crüsemann there is a clear difference between the hymn and the thanksgiving. Working from a form-critical analysis, he holds that the thanksgiving of an individual is a totally independent category in which the psalmist addresses God directly and tells others of his works in the setting of a thanksgiving liturgy.[5] H. H. Guthrie has pointed out that, unlike the hymn, the thanksgiving uses verbs that are recitative or narrative in form. They announce what God has done for a specific suppliant in a specific situation. For Guthrie, moreover, the theology of the hymn is completely different. Hymns are acclamations of the god's nature on the basis of the regular occurrences in the cycles of nature. But thanksgivings are the expression of a person's specific experience of the nature of Yahweh. Thus a communal

---

[2] See C. Westermann, *Praise and Lament*, 25-30; "Psalms, Book of," *IDBSup*, 707.

[3] C. Westermann, *Praise and Lament*, 31.

[4] See W. Brueggemann, "Psalms and the Life of Faith," 9.

[5] See F. Crüsemann, *Studien zum Formgeschichte*, 210-284.

thanksgiving "is used by people to offer praise to a God whose character was manifest in the rescue from oppression of a band of slaves."[6] In the final analysis Guthrie's study of thanksgivings or psalms of declarative praise is essentially a way of doing theology. It has to do with the concrete experience of divine intervention and its fitting expression in liturgy. The focus of that liturgy is a God of surprises, not an ancient Near Eastern deity of stability.

The structure of the thanksgiving or psalm of declarative praise normally consists of three elements: (a) introduction or call to praise/thank; (b) an account of the newness that Yahweh has brought forth; (c) conclusion which is usually a renewed call to praise/thank.[7]

Psalm 118[8]

> O give thanks to the LORD,
>   for he is good;
> his steadfast love endures for ever!
> [3]Let the house of Aaron say,
>   "His steadfast love endures for ever."
> [4]Let those who fear the LORD say,
>   "His steadfast love endures for ever."
>
> [5]Out of my distress I called on the LORD;
>   the LORD answered me and set me free.
> [6]With the LORD on my side I do not fear.
>   What can man do to me?
> [7]The LORD is on my side to help me;
>   I shall look in triumph on those who hate me.
> [8]It is better to take refuge in the LORD
>   than to put confidence in man.

---

[6]H. H. Guthrie, *Theology as Thanksgiving*, 25. In his earlier work (*Israel's Sacred Songs*, 150-151) Guthrie had already pointed out this fundamental difference between the hymn and the thanksgiving.

[7]See C. Westermann, *Praise and Lament*, 85-86, 103-104; "Psalms, Book of,"*IDBSup*, 707.

[8]See A. Weiser, *The Psalms*, 722-730; H. –J. Kraus, *Psalmen*, 800-809; H. H. Guthrie, *Israel's Sacred Songs*, 152-156.

[9]It is better to take refuge in the LORD
    than to put confidence in princes.
[10]All nations surrounded me;
    in the name of the LORD I cut them off!
[11]They surrounded me, surrounded me on every side;
    in the name of the LORD I cut them off!
[12]They surrounded me like bees,
    they blazed like a fire of thorns;
    in the name of the LORD I cut them off!
[13]I was pushed hard, so that I was falling,
    but the LORD helped me.
[14]The LORD is my strength and my song;
    he has become my salvation.
[15]Hark, glad songs of victory
    in the tents of the righteous:
    "The right hand of the LORD does valiantly,
[16]the right hand of the LORD is exalted,
    the right hand of the LORD does valiantly!"
[17]I shall not die, but I shall live,
    and recount the deeds of the LORD.
[18]The LORD has chastened me sorely,
    but he has not given me over to death.

[19]Open to me the gates of righteousness,
    that I may enter through them
    and give thanks to the LORD.

[20]This is the gate of the LORD;
    the righteous shall enter through it.

[21]I thank thee that thou hast answered me
    and hast become my salvation.
[22]The stone which the builders rejected
    has become the head of the corner.
[23]This is the LORD's doing;
    it is marvelous in our eyes.
[24]This is the day which the LORD has made;
    let us rejoice and be glad in it.

[25]Save us, we beseech thee, O LORD!
O LORD, we beseech thee, give us success!

[26]Blessed be he who enters in the name of the LORD!
We bless you from the house of the LORD.

[27]The LORD is God, and he has given us light.
Bind the festal procession with branches,
up to the horns of the altar!

[28]Thou art my God, and I will give thanks to thee:
thou art my God, I will extol thee.

[29]O give thanks to the LORD, for he is good;
for his steadfast love endures for ever!

The "I" of this psalm is often identified as a king who has experienced social upheaval or some form of political unrest.[9] Having overcome the problem through Yahweh's gracious intervention, he sings of this newness in a thanksgiving or psalm of declarative praise. The guests invited to the liturgy of the thanksgiving offering[10] are the whole congregation of Israel. The psalm may be divided as follows: (a) opening invitation to liturgical praise (vv 1-4); (b) thanksgiving song of the king (vv 5-21); (c) liturgical dialogue of approach (vv 22-29).

The deliverance of the king is not a private affair since the nation's well-being is tied up with his person. In the opening invitation the psalmist sings of Yahweh's sense of covenant commitment (v 1: "good," "steadfast love") and then calls on the congregation to join in celebrating Yahweh's graciousness to the king. The Israelites (v 2), the priests (v 3), and the proselytes (v 4: "those who fear the Lord") announce that Yahweh is indeed a faithful and loyal God. In verses 5-9 the poet begins to describe his former state of disorientation. He cried out in his peril and Yahweh

[9]See S. Mowinckel, *The Psalms in Israel's Worship*, 1. 180.

[10]See R. de Vaux, *Ancient Israel*, 417-418; *Studies in Old Testament Sacrifice* (Cardiff: University of Wales, 1964) 31-33.

responded (v 5). To experience Yahweh's presence is to be able to vanquish any human obstacles (vv 6-7). To resort to Yahweh is far better than to place confidence in mere humans (vv 8-9). In verses 10-14 the king recites the account of the danger which made it imperative for him to cry out. The danger is associated with all nations (v 10), those cosmic powers which are ever anxious to upset harmony and balance in the world. They were like bees and a fire of thorns but they did not win the day owing to Yahweh's name and hence person (v 12). When the king's strength was failing, Yahweh stepped in. Salvation means Yahweh's faithful response in the midst of seemingly insuperable odds (vv 13-14).

The king's escape is now the occasion for the people's exultation. They take up the song of Yahweh's victorious right hand (vv 15-16). Actually they are celebrating much more than an isolated case of divine intervention. When the king was threatened with death (vv 17-18), their own world was threatened with upheaval and disruption. Death is the apt term for the state of disorientation. In verse 19 the king now asks to enter the sanctuary since he has experienced Yahweh's vindication ("righteousness"). After the priest's affirmative answer in verse 20 the king formally proclaims the message of newness in verse 21: "I thank thee that thou hast answered me and hast become my salvation."

In verses 22-25 the people articulate their sense of bewilderment and amazement. The stone rejected by the builders has become nothing less than the cornerstone (v 22). This is indeed a world of radical reversals — only Yahweh can be responsible for this surprising turn of events (v 23). It is the appropriate time for celebration and hence further requests for deliverance (vv 24-25).

As the liturgical dialogue continues, the priests now pronounce a blessing over both the king and the assembly and bid them to approach to the very horns of the altar (vv 26-27) to participate in the sacrifice. Fittingly the king addresses his message of praise to Yahweh once more (v 28). In keeping with the introduction of the psalm, it is a message which the people are to proclaim as well (v 29). Goodness is always a treasure to be shared with others.

At prayer we must make God's gift-giving our own contagious experience.[11] Like the people in the psalm, we are to be touched by God's graciousness to others. Whenever disease, hatred, unemployment, loneliness, and despair give way to health, love, a job, community, and hope, we must join in the chorus. They were once the construction rejects but now they are edifying testimony to a concerned God who likes to surprise us, assuring us that despite rumors to the contrary he is alive and well. Unfortunately we humans find it relatively easy to praise our God's gift-giving. It is the graciousness of our fellow humans that is difficult to acknowledge. Yet at prayer we can find a God who bewilders and amazes us with his gifted humans who make possible the trek to reorientation for others. They are so often the little people who visit nursing homes, who care for the down and out, who console the bereaved. "Amazing grace" is present here. Prayer is the fitting moment to confess that presence and sing of a God who seldom chooses to effect his surprises completely alone.

Psalm 118 is a challenge to our prayer life in another direction. It makes us aware of the rejects in our own life (v 22). They are the living dead (vv 17-18), the mute monuments to our inhumanity. Prayer is the call to a liturgy of rehabilitation whereby the rejects can recover their self-esteem and thereby reflect a God of surprises. Our eucharistic prayer especially is that dangerous assembly where we promise to be food and drink for others. Eucharist is the prayer which pulls together the pain of rejection and the thrill of transformation in the passion-death-resurrection event of Jesus. To approach the horns of this altar (v 27)

---

[11] For M. Luther's appropriation of Psalm 118 see R. Hals, "Psalm 118," *Int* 37 (1983) 277-283.

means to leave the sanctuary in search of the rejects. Eucharist is to be the stimulus for radical gift-giving.

Psalm 30[12]

> I will extol thee, O LORD, for thou has drawn me up,
>   and hast not let my foes rejoice over me.
> [2]O LORD my God, I cried to thee for help,
>   and thou hast healed me.
>
> [3]O LORD, thou hast brought up my soul from Sheol,
>   restored me to life from among those gone down to the
> Pit.
>
> [4]Sing praises to the LORD, O you his saints,
>   and give thanks to his holy name.
> [5]For his anger is but for a moment, and his favor is for a
> lifetime.
>   Weeping may tarry for the night, but joy comes with
> the morning.
>
> [6]As for me, I said in my prosperity,
>   "I shall never be moved."
> [7]By thy favor, O LORD,
>   thou hadst established me as a strong mountain;
>   thou didst hide thy face, I was dismayed.
>
> [8]To thee, O LORD, I cried;
>   and to the LORD I made supplication:
> [9]"What profit is there in my death,
>   if I go down to the Pit?
> Will the dust praise thee?
>   Will it tell of thy faithfulness?
> [10]Hear, O LORD, and be gracious to me!
>   O LORD, be thou my helper!"

[12]See A. Weiser, *The Psalms*, 265-273; H. – J. Kraus, *Psalmen*, 240-244; C. Westermann, *Praise and Lament*, 102-106.

¹¹Thou hast turned for me my mourning into dancing;
thou hast loosed my sackcloth
and girded me with gladness,
¹²that my soul may praise thee and not be silent.
O LORD my God, I will give thanks to thee for ever.

This psalm is an individual's expression of divine deliverance from suffering and distress. Although the psalmist speaks about death, "The body of a thanksgiving quite often contains hyperbole in which the deliverance accomplished by the god is likened to rescue from death and annihilation themselves . . ."¹³ The psalm may be divided as follows: (a) praise of Yahweh for having delivered the person from his distress (v 1); (b) the recounting of his experience (vv 2-3); (c) invitation to those present to praise Yahweh and learn from his experience (vv 4-5); (d) more explicit description of the plight (vv 6-11); (e) conclusion (v 12).

L. Alonso Schökel has shown that the artistry of the poet consists, not in simple repetition, but in the development of new elements as the psalm progresses. Verse 1 speaks of the psalmist's liberation. However, in the next four verses the author situates supplication before liberation and places thanksgiving after liberation. In verse 2a the psalmist cries out for help. In verses 2b-3 he experiences liberation, viz., he was healed and brought up from Sheol. Then in verses 4-5 the psalmist takes up the theme of thanksgiving, calling upon the bystanders to take up the chorus of praise and learn from his experience. God's graciousness must be celebrated. At this point the psalmist introduces a new element in the supplication-liberation-thanksgiving schema — it is the fall. In verses 6-7 the psalmist mentions that he was overconfident and that he was consequently

¹³ H. H. Guthrie, *Theology as Thanksgiving*, 8.

¹⁴See L. Alonso Schökel, "Psalm 30 as Christian Prayer," *Homiletic and Pastoral Review* 72 (1972) 22-27; *Treinta Salmos*, 133-145.

stricken with some distress. In verses 8-10 he takes up the supplication again, noting that God would gain nothing from his death. In verse 11, he develops the liberation — the giftedness of the new situation. The removal of sackcloth and the dance are evidence of reorientation. Finally in verse 12 he once again accentuates the duty of thanksgiving: abrupt newness must be communicated.

There are two polarities that govern the psalm, viz., life and death. In verses 3b and 9a death is symbolized by going down, viz., into the Pit. In verses 5b and 9b death is symbolized by silence (weeping and the absence of praise). In verse 3a life is described in terms of bringing up, viz., from Sheol, and in verse 2a in terms of healing. In verses 1a, 4, 5b, and 12 the silence of death is vanquished by singing. In this psalm there is an ascending direction: (a) from death to life; (b) from sickness to health; (c) from punishment (the hidden face in verse 7) to joy; (d) from night to morning (v 5b).

At prayer we sometimes take uncanny delight in preferring death to life, sickness to health, punishment to joy, night to morning. The great failures are always before our eyes: the alcoholics, the drug addicts, the spendthrifts, etc. All too easily they remind us of the psalmist: "Foolish me, I said when things were going well for me, 'I shall never be overwhelmed by chaos!' Yahweh, because it pleased you, you made me like a strong mountain; but when you weren't blessing me, I fell all apart" (vv 6-7).[15] Prayer, however, must challenge us to reflect on life, health, joy, and morning. We are asked to remember the rehabilitated and reformed — ample proof that there is indeed a God of surprises. We must hear their testimony, applaud their efforts, and share in the happiness of their reorientation. Why must we prefer sackcloth to dancing shoes (v 11)?[16]

---

[15] H. H. Guthrie (*Theology as Thanksgiving*, 7) is the author of this translation.

[16] For the hermeneutical aspect of Psalm 30 see T. Wahl, "Praying Israel's Psalms Responsibly as Christians: An Exercise in Hermeneutic," *Worship* 54 (1980) 386-396.

Prayer must also turn us in the direction of those who still yearn for reorientation but have not yet achieved it. Why should death have the last word (v 9)? In the context of covenant they cry to us: "'Be thou my helper!'" (v 10). The God of surprises truly deserves that title when he enlists humans in this enterprise of mutual help. The distressing question at prayer must be: after the cry for help who will be the source of healing (v 2)? To the extent that others experience misery, we are in Sheol, the Pit. Our celebration of reorientation in the Father's raising up of Jesus by sending the Spirit must lead us to make hope possible for the less than beautiful people. Insofar as we extricate them from Sheol, the Pit, to that extent we can join in Paul's celebrative chorus: "'Death is swallowed up in victory. O death, where is thy victory? O death, where is thy sting?'" (1 Cor 15:54-55).

Psalm 40[17]

> I waited patiently for the LORD;
>> he inclined to me and heard my cry.
> [2]He drew me up from the desolate pit,
>> out of the miry bog,
>> and set my feet upon a rock, making my steps secure.
> [3]He put a new song in my mouth,
>> a song of praise to our God.
> Many will see and fear,
>> and put their trust in the LORD.
>
> [4]Blessed is the man who makes the LORD his trust,
>> who does not turn to the proud,
>>> to those who go astray after false gods!
>
> [5]Thou hast multiplied, O LORD my God,
>> thy wondrous deeds and thy thoughts toward us;
>> none can compare with thee!

---

[17] See A. Weiser, *The Psalms*, 331-341; H. –J. Kraus, *Psalmen*, 305-310; C. Westermann, *Praise and Lament*, 103-105.

Were I to proclaim and tell of them,
    they would be more than can be numbered.

⁶Sacrifice and offering thou dost not desire;
    but thou hast given me an open ear.
Burnt offering and sin offering thou hast not required.
⁷Then I said, "Lo, I come;
    in the roll of the book it is written of me;
⁸I delight to do thy will, O my God;
    thy law is within my heart."

⁹I have told the glad news of deliverance
    in the great congregation;
lo, I have not restrained my lips,
    as thou knowest, O LORD.
¹⁰I have not hid thy saving help within my heart,
    I have spoken of thy faithfulness and thy salvation;
I have not concealed why steadfast love and thy
    faithfulness from the great congregation.

¹¹Do not thou, O LORD, withhold thy mercy from me,
    let thy steadfast love and thy faithfulness
        ever preserve me!
¹²For evils have encompassed me without number;
    my iniquities have overtaken me, till I cannot see;
they are more than the hairs of my head;
    my heart fails me.

¹³Be pleased, O LORD, to deliver me!
    O LORD, make haste to help me!
¹⁴Let them be put to shame and confusion altogether
    who seek to snatch away my life;
let them be turned back and brought to dishonor
    who desire my hurt!
¹⁵Let them be appalled because of their shame
    who say to me, "Aha, Aha!"

¹⁶But may all who seek thee
    rejoice and be glad in thee;

> may those who love thy salvation
>   say continually, "Great is the LORD!"
> [17]As for me, I am poor and needy;
>   but the Lord takes thought for me.
> Thou art my help and my deliverer;
>   do not tarry, O my God!

This psalm initially strikes us as being odd. After the joyful mood of the thanksgiving in verses 1-11 there is the apparently unjustified switch to the somber mood of the lament in verses 13-17. Even within the thanksgiving the teaching about true sacrifice (vv 6-8) seems to impede the psalmist's praise of Yahweh in verses 5 and 9. To make matters worse, verses 13-17 are repeated with only slight variations in Psalm 70.

Though Psalm 40 continues to be the focus of scholarly attention, the following proposal seems reasonable.[18] A pre-existing lament was fused with a thanksgiving to create a new psalm. When this fusion occurred, other changes were introduced. There were additions from wisdom circles (v 4) and prophetic circles (vv 6-8). Finally in order to smooth over the transition from the thanksgiving to the lament, verse 12 was introduced. The result is a new prayer, perhaps reflecting the period prior to the reconstruction of the Second Temple (hence before 520-515 B. C.). The psalm may be divided as follows: (a) introduction (v 1); (b) account of Yahweh's deliverance (vv 2-3); (c) instruction and praise (vv 4-5); (d) meaning of true sacrifice (vv 6-8); (e) expression of gratitude (vv 9-10); (f) conclusion of thanksgiving (v 11); (g) transitional link (v 12); (h) individual lament (vv 13-17 = Psalm 70).

In verses 1-2 the psalmist sings of release from death, perhaps from some serious illness. Here he contrasts the

---

[18]On this proposal see C. Stuhlmueller, *Psalms*, 1. 216. G. Braulik (Psalm 40 und der Gottesknecht Forschung zur Bibel 18; Würzburg; Echter, 1975) holds that verses 1-11 are a psalm of professed faith while verses 13-17 are a psalm of supplication rather than lament.

precariousness of his situation (v 2: "desolate pit," "miry bog") with divine security (v 2: "rock, making my steps secure"). This complete reversal leads into an expression of his new state — there is a new song in his mouth (v 3). At this juncture the wisdom addition in verse 4 is a beatitude reflecting the desirable state of those who lean on Yahweh and not on idolators. Yahweh is simply incomparable — it is impossible to praise him enough (v 5). In verses 6-8 the psalm echoes the nature of genuine sacrifice as reflected in Israel's prophets who inveighed against mechanical liturgy.[19] Without denigrating ritual (the setting is the sanctuary!), this section stresses the essence of sacrifice, viz., listening and acting in faith. The law in the psalmist's heart (v 8) smacks of Jeremiah's insistence on the new covenant (see Jer 31:31-34). In verses 9-10 the psalmist attests that Yahweh's gracious disruption in his life has not been a miser's booty but the patrimony of the community. Finally in verse 11 the psalmist concludes by asking for Yahweh's ongoing covenant commitment.

Verse 12 is the transitional verse to the lament proper which accentuates the utter powerlessness of the suppliant. There is a note of urgency in that he pleads for quick and decisive action (vv 13,17). The psalmist vents his anger by praying for the downfall of all those who have conspired against him (vv 14-15). However, verse 16 indicates that the psalmist is seeking Yahweh more than the overthrow of his enemies. But release from his present ordeal is certainly not being disparaged.

At prayer, especially liturgical prayer we must be overwhelmed by a theology which links worship and interhuman concern. Liturgy cannot be our flight from the disorientation which daily attends our world. Liturgy must be the awareness of our God's presence which impels us to those

---

[19] Some of these prophetic texts are the following: Isa 1:10-17; Hos 6:4-6; Amos 5:21-27; Mic 6:6-8. On the prophetic critique of purely mechanical liturgy see J. F. Craghan, "The Book of Hosea — A Survey of Recent Literature on the First of the Minor Prophets," *BTB* 1 (1971) 153-154.

people and those situations where our God's absence is most conspicuous. Liturgy must announce our resolution to bring about reorientation. In H. H. Guthrie's expression the God of the Bible puts "priority on involvement with a human, historical community rather than on protection of divine purity. That is why the humblest participant in the *todah* (thanksgiving) cult is more closely in touch with God than is the pretender to high, theological wisdom."[20]

In the final analysis the fusion of the thanksgiving and the lament is a felicitous commentary on our prayer situation. Our community consists both of those who have joyfully announced Yahweh's gift-giving and of those who poignantly bemoan Yahweh's reluctance to give. Prayer must lead us to "rejoice with those who rejoice, weep with those who weep" (Rom 12:15). Prayer is a many-splendored enterprise.

Psalm 73[21]

> Truly God is good to the upright,
>   to those who are pure in heart.
> [2]But as for me, my feet had almost stumbled,
>   my steps had well nigh slipped.
> [3]For I was envious of the arrogant,
>   when I saw the prosperity of the wicked.
>
> [4]For they have no pangs; their bodies are sound and sleek.
> [5]They are not in trouble as other men are;
>   they are not stricken like other men.
> [6]Therefore pride is their necklace;
>   violence covers them as a garment.
> [7]Their eyes swell out with fatness,
>   their hearts overflow with follies.
> [8]They scoff and speak with malice;
>   loftily they threaten oppression.

---

[20] H. H. Guthrie, *Theology as Thanksgiving*, 70.
[21] See A. Weiser, *The Psalms*, 505-516; H.–J. Kraus, *Psalmen*, 501-511.

⁹They set their mouths against the heavens,
    and their tongue struts through the earth.
¹⁰Therefore the people turn and praise them;
    and find no fault in them.
¹¹And they say, "How can God know?
    Is there knowledge in the Most High?"
¹²Behold, these are the wicked;
    always at ease, they increase in riches.
¹³All in vain have I kept my heart clean
    and washed my hands in innocence.
¹⁴For all the day long I have been stricken,
    and chastened every morning.

¹⁵If I had said, "I will speak thus,"
    I would have been untrue to the generation of thy
children.
¹⁶But when I thought how to understand this,
    it seemed to me a wearisome task,
¹⁷until I went into the sanctuary of God;
    then I perceived their end.
¹⁸Truly thou dost set them in slippery places;
    thou dost make them fall to ruin.
¹⁹How they are destroyed in a moment,
    swept away utterly by terrors!
²⁰They are like a dream when one awakes,
    on awaking you despise their phantoms.

²¹When my soul was embittered,
    when I was pricked in heart,
²²I was stupid and ignorant,
    I was like a beast toward thee.
²³Nevertheless I am continually with thee;
    thou dost hold my right hand.
²⁴Thou dost guide me with thy counsel,
    and afterward thou wilt receive me to glory.
²⁵Whom have I in heaven but thee?
    And there is nothing upon earth that I desire besides
thee.

²⁶My flesh and my heart may fail,
   but God is the strength of my heart and my portion for
   ever?²⁷For lo, those who are far from thee shall perish;

   thou dost put an end to those who are false to thee.
²⁸But for me it is good to be near God;
   I have made the Lord GOD my refuge,
   that I may tell of all thy works.

For a number of authors this psalm is classified as a wisdom psalm.²² For others it is a mixture of psalm types.²³ However, R. E. Murphy has suggested that wisdom content is not a sufficient criterion, adding: " . . . in literary style this poem resembles more a thanksgiving song; it begins with a conclusion that is the reason for the poet's grateful prayer (v 1) . . ."²⁴ It is the psalm's insistence on radical newness, therefore, which accounts for its place here as a thanksgiving or psalm of declarative praise. It may be divided as follows: (a) anticipated conclusion (v 1); (b) the prosperity of the arrogant wicked (vv 2-12); (c) temptation and new perception (vv 13-17); (d) the fate of the wicked (vv 18-22); (e) the fate of the good (vv 23-28).²⁵

After the anticipated conclusion (v 1) the psalmist takes up the classical problem of retribution: the evil prosper while the good perish. This is clearly the poet's painful stage of disorientation. In verses 4-5 he emphasizes the sound health of the wicked. In verses 6-7 he describes their pre-

---

²²See B. W. Anderson, *Out of the Depths*, 151; L. G. Perdue, *Wisdom and Cult*, 286-287; S. Terrien, *The Elusive Presence*, 315-316; L. Alonso Schökel, *Treinta Salmos*, 275; L. C. Allen, "Psalm 73: An Analysis," *TB* 33 (1982) 93-118.

²³See H. –J. Kraus, *Psalmen*, 503-504.   J. F. Ross ("Psalm 73," *Israelite Wisdom: Theological and Literary Essays in Honor of Samuel Terrien* [ed. J. G. Gammie et al.; Missoula, Montana: Scholars Press, 1978] 170) concludes: "Psalm 73 is *both* a wisdom psalm *and* a psalm of lament, trust, and thanksgiving." (author's italics)

²⁴R. E. Murphy, "A Consideration of the Classification 'Wisdom Psalms,'" 164.

²⁵This structure is fundamentally that proposed by L. Alonso Schökel (*Treinta Salmos*, 277-282). For different structural conceptions see L. G. Perdue, *Wisdom and Cult*, 287-288; J. F. Ross, "Psalm 73," 163-165.

sumptuousness and violence. In verses 8-9 he moves on to their innate scorn and derision. In verses 10-11 he registers the effect of these arrogant wicked on the believing Israelite. Instead of labelling such practices as opposed to covenant, the believer is hoodwinked, becoming a convert to their blasphemy. Verse 12 summarizes his painfully acquired observations.

In verses 13-14 the psalmist candidly exposes his own temptation. He is tempted to regard his fidelity as utterly senseless. The torments tend to add conviction to the position of the arrogant wicked. But to have given in would have meant to be unfaithful to Israel's faith (v 15). His failure to understand (v 16) was necessary so that he could open up to a new vision (v 17). This is the moment of reorientation, for this vision is not his own achievement but a gift.[26] It is significant that God nowhere speaks in the psalm. However, it is in the process of meditation that the psalmist discovers the personal presence of his God. As S. Terrien puts it, "The psalmist did not offer any intellectual solution to the problem of evil, but it was the intellectual consideration of this problem which stirred his religious consciousness and led him to receive the dispensation of a new truth."[27]

In verses 18-22 the psalmist examines the real fate of the wicked and criticizes his earlier temptation. He perceives that evil will not have the last word. This God does not sit idly by.   He sets them on a slippery path so that in a brief period of time they will be utterly devastated (vv 18-20). At this point the psalmist recalls his earlier frame of mind which made him like a beast (vv 21-22). What is significant in this section is that the poet for the first time addresses Yahweh as "thou."[28] This is the gift whereby he becomes

[26]See L. Alonso Schökel, *Treinta Salmos*, 276. J. F. Ross ("Psalm 73," 167-169) translates "santuaries" rather than "sanctuary" in verse 17. He holds that the psalmist's visit to the sanctuaries of God was not only to the temple proper but to those buildings where Israel's sages discussed problems of theodicy.

[27]S. Terrien, *The Elusive Presence*, 316.

[28]Ibid.

aware of his God's presence. He does not ponder a theological problem in solitude. Rather, he opens himself up to accept the gratuitous presence of this God. Theological problems must be aired in community.

In the conclusion the poet develops his new level of being. Yahweh holds him, guides him, and receives him in honor (vv 23-24; RSV offers "honor" as a variant to "glory" in verse 24). There is really no one else who matters in heaven or on earth (v 25). Regardless of what happens to his physical well-being, Yahweh is his constant support (v 26). In the concluding verses the poet contrasts distance from and nearness to God. It is this nearness which prompts him to share Yahweh's gift-giving with others.

Although some find an afterlife in the conclusion of the poem,[29] it is also possible that the intensity of the poem leads to an ambiguous statement of future security. As Alonso Schökel describes it,[30] the psalmist does realize that he is not simply another phenomenon of time and space. He enjoys an intimate, though not totally unimpaired, vision of his God.

At prayer we must be willing to accept the presence of our God as a gift. Our limitations which are often at the root of our disorientation need not add to that state by way of revolt or despair. Reorientation can also be the presence of Another who invites us to think in terms of persons, not problems. Prayer must lead us to accept the embrace of our God, not simply a substitute to control our intellectual and emotional imbalance. In the words of Terrien, "An inquisitive essay has become a prayer . . . He inserted his doubt into the context of his adoration."[31]

Prayer must also be our support in seeking answers to the dangers of our nuclear world with its exploitation of

[29] See M. Dahood, *Psalms 51-100*, 187-188, 194-196.

[30] L. Alonso Schökel, *Treinta Salmos*, 284. See also J. F. Ross, "Psalm 73," 175, #92.

[31] S. Terrien, *The Elusive Presence*, 316.

humans. Prayer is to be our catalyst for asking hard questions, even if the answers are not immediately forthcoming. Reorientation does not merely mean that we have resolved all problems. It also implies that we leave behind the secure but false solutions of the past and in the presence of our God embark on a new venture of answers. "Theology that is vital stands on the boundary between the old theology which has been systematized and the new theology which must be formulated. And if man's intellect is to be brought into the sanctuary of God, this standing on the boundary between the old and the new is imperative."[32]

Psalm 124[33]

> If it had not been the LORD who was on our side,
>   let Israel now say—
> [2]if it had not been the LORD who was on our side,
>   when men rose up against us,
> [3]then they would have swallowed us up alive,
>   when their anger was kindled against us;
> [4]then the flood would have swept us away,
>   the torrent would have gone over us;
> [5]then over us would have gone the raging waters.
> [6]Blessed be the LORD,
>   who has not given us as prey to their teeth!
> [7]We have escaped as a bird from the snare of the fowlers;
>   the snare is broken, and we have escaped!
>
> [8]Our help is in the name of the LORD,
>   who made heaven and earth.

This communal thanksgiving or psalm of declarative praise offers no precise clues as to its setting. Hence there is no specific national emergency such as the fall of Jerusalem. In any event it was some great debacle from which Yahweh

---

[32] B. W. Anderson, *Out of the Depths*, 156-157.

[33] See A. Weiser, *The Psalms*, 754-756; H. -J. Kraus, *Psalmen*, 846-849; C. Westermann, *Praise and Lament*, 83-88.

delivered the community. Alonso Schökel[34] describes the psalm as a first expression in the wake of some violent upheaval which leaves the community trembling. Yet this trembling attests to the fact that life goes on. It is precisely in this experience that God's activity is revealed. This is, therefore, an intense religious experience that acknowledges the theology of grace. At the conclusion of the psalm the agitation dies down, giving way to a statement of exclusive confidence in Yahweh. The psalm may be divided as follows: (a) reflections on the national emergency (vv 1-5); (b) Yahweh's deliverance (vv 6-7); (c) praise of the Creator's intervention (v8).

The imagery of disorientation begins with the mention of humans rising up against the community (v 2). The poet then develops the peril by perhaps alluding to the battle against the powers of chaos and to the primeval flood. In verse 3 the adversaries are depicted as sea-monsters who in their fury are anxious to swallow up Yahweh's people. In verses 4-5 the enemies are raging waters after the manner of the primeval waters that threaten to inundate the community. For the poet the danger is eminently real.

The imagery of liberation or reorientation is found in verses 6-7. The people were not handed over as prey to the enemies' ravenous teeth. Positively they enjoyed the sense of freedom which the bird experiences in escaping from the fowlers' snare. The breaking of the snare is the break for freedom.

Verse 8 brings together creation, the divine name, and the experience of deliverance. The Creator bearing a personal name demonstrates a personal interest in this people. Israel's experience attests, not to a cosmic deity of the ancient Near East but to one "who chose to be involved and active in the events constituting the life and history of a people, . . ."[35] The outcome of this intervention is that God's people can face the

---

[34] L. Alsonso Schökel, *Treinta Salmos*, 378.

[35] H. H. Guthrie, *Theology as Thanksgiving*, 22. Guthrie goes on (pp. 25-30) to discuss hymn and thanksgiving as the mix out of which Israel did theology.

future with renewed confidence because of this transformational event. Thanksgiving is the only adequate expression of the transformation.

At community prayer we must recall those transforming events when prejudice, oppression, and manipulation — our modern version of the powers of chaos — were significantly overcome. We must celebrate the goodness of those people whose self-giving ways brought about the breaking of the snare (v 7). Prayer is to be the proper occasion for our communal acknowledgement of such successes. The truly human community celebrates here and now the great exploits of its members, considering the encomiums of eulogies too late indeed. To recognize now the gifts of fellow humans is to recognize the Giver par excellence.

At the same time prayer must move our community to set the stage for future expressions of thanksgiving. At prayer we must realize those chaotic powers that still oppress fellow humans. Prayer means the setting in motion of that vast machinery that will serve to demolish the new sea-monsters. In reacting to the resurgence of chaos, our God chooses to associate with the seemingly frail so that the song of thanksgiving may be made possible for countless others. To experience reorientation is to provide reorientation for others. To receive a gift is to give a gift.

New Testament

Matthew 21:33-43

33"Hear another parable. There was a householder who planted a vineyard, and set a hedge around it, and dug a wine press in it, and built a tower, and let it out to tenants, and went into another country. 34When the season of fruit drew near, he sent his servants to the tenants, to get his fruit; 35and the tenants took his servants and beat one, killed another, and stoned another. 36Again he sent other servants, more than the first; and they did the same to them. [37]Afterward he sent his son to them, saying, 'They will respect my son.' [38]But when the tenants saw the son, they said to themselves, 'This is the heir; come, let us kill him and have his inheritance.' [39]And they took him and cast him out of the vineyard, and killed him. [40]When therefore the owner of the vineyard comes, what will he do to those tenants?" [41]They said to him, "He will put those wretches to a miserable death, and let out the vineyard to other tenants who will give him the fruits in their seasons."

[42]Jesus said to them, "Have you never read in the scriptures:

'The very stone which the builders rejected
has become the head of the corner;
this was the Lord's doing,
and it is marvelous in our eyes'?

[43]Therefore I tell you, the kingdom of God will be taken away from you and given to a nation producing the fruits of it."

It is possible that the original parable of the unjust tenant farmers concluded with verse 39. Thus Jesus would have recounted the rather upsetting story of Galilean background. A landowner did not get his due share of the harvest from his tenant farmers. After two futile attempts (the sending of servants and still more servants) the landowner sent his son. However, taking advantage of the son's status as heir, the tenant farmers murdered him.

Christian tradition added material from Isaiah's song of the vineyard (Isa 5:1-7): the planting of the vineyard (v 33) and the question (v 40). Christian tradition also interpreted the son as Jesus. At this point the movement of disorientation-reorientation became central. Since death was not God's last word with regard to his Son's fate, the Christian community went on to speak of his exaltation.

Appropriately that community cited Ps 118:22-23 (v 42 — see also Acts 4:11; 1 Pet 2:7). Owing to the Father's intervention the rejected stone eventually became the cornerstone. For the Christian community Jesus' original parable of a disconcerting affair in Galilee became an allegory of disorientation-reorientation, viz., human violence offset by divine intervention.[36]

At prayer the resurrection of Jesus must be our central paradigm of reorientation. This event was not resuscitation but transformation.[37] Hence Jesus was on a new level of being. By his willingness to challenge the old securities and thereby accept death he was made capable of a new type of life. At prayer we cannot simply say that Jesus regained everything he had surrendered at the moment of the incarnation, since that would be to disregard his life, especially as it culminated in passion and death. The Risen Lord attains reorientation only at the cost of disorientation. It is this gift-giving of Jesus that makes possible the gift-giving of the Father. To applaud the Father's gift is to let go of our focus on self and make Christ the center of our lives. It is this centrality that makes possible new empty tombs and third day activities. Easter is an essential ingredient of all prayer.

Luke 15:11-32

> [11]And he said, "There was a man who had two sons; [12]and the younger of them said to his father, 'Father, give me the share of property that falls to me.' And he divided his living between them. [13]Not many days later, the younger son gathered all he had and took his journey into a far country, and there he squandered his property in loose living. [14]And when he had spent everything, a great famine arose in that country, and he began to be in want.

---

[36]See J. P. Meier, *Matthew*, 243-245; *The Vision of Matthew: Christ, Church, and Morality in the First Gospel* (New York: Paulist, 1979) 150-152.

[37]See F. X. Durrwell, *The Resurrection*, 148-150; R. E. Brown, *The Virginal Conception and Bodily Resurrection of Jesus* (New York: Paulist, 1973) 72-73.

15So he went and joined himself to one of the citizens of that country, who sent him into his fields to feed swine. 16And he would gladly have fed on the pods that the swine ate; and no one gave him anything. 17But when he came to himself he said, 'How many of my father's hired servants have bread enough and to spare, but I perish here with hunger! 18I will arise and go to my father, and I will say to him, "Father, I have sinned against heaven and before you; 19I am no longer worthy to be called your son; treat me as one of your hired servants."' 20And he arose and came to his father. But while he was yet at a distance, his father saw him and had compassion, and ran and embraced him and kissed him. 21And the son said to him, 'Father, I have sinned against heaven and before you; I am no longer worthy to be called your son.' 22But the father said to his servants, 'Bring quickly the best robe, and put it on him; and put a ring on his hand, and shoes on his feet; 23and bring the fatted calf and kill it, and let us eat and make merry; 24for this my son was dead, and is alive again; he was lost, and is found.' And they began to make merry.

25"Now his elder son was in the field; and as he came and drew near to the house, he heard music and dancing. 26And he called one of the servants and asked what this meant. 27And he said to him, 'Your brother has come, and your father has killed the fatted calf, because he has received him safe and sound.' 28But he was angry and refused to go in. His father came out and entreated him, 29but he answered his father, 'Lo, these many years I have served you, and I never disobeyed your command; yet you never gave me a kid, that I might make merry with my friends. 30But when this son of yours came, who has devoured your living with harlots, you killed for him the fatted calf!' 31And he said to him, 'Son, you are always with me, and all that is mine is yours. 32It was fitting to make merry and be glad, for this your brother was dead, and is alive; he was lost, and is found.'"

Taken merely by itself, this parable falls into two parts:
(a) the departure and return of the younger son (vv 11-24);
and (b) the protest of the elder son (vv 25-32). Both parts end
with the same saying ("make merry," "dead/alive," "lost-
/found"). Jesus challenges his audience to imagine the discrepancy: the renegade son at the father's party and the
obedient son refusing to join the party. "One feels understanding for the position of all three protagonists, but in the
end the parable shows a prodigal son inside feasting and a
dutiful son outside pouting."[38]

As part of Luke's redaction, the parable is preceded by an
introduction (vv 1-2) and two other parables, viz., the lost
sheep (vv 3-7) and the lost coin (vv 8-10). In this setting Jesus
is presented as one who receives sinners in God's name
simply because they are lost (sheep, coin, son). On the other
hand, the Pharisees and the scribes (v 2) are now depicted as
the elder brother of the Prodigal.[39] For Luke Jesus' divine
forgiveness and divine joy is the theme of his parables here.
"'Joy to be shared here and now' is the good news and the
unifying dynamic theme of this chapter — whether it be
presented as the joy of the father at the reunion banquet or
the joy of the shepherd and the woman who invite others in
humbler circumstances. It is the joy of Jesus Himself as he
gathers in and welcomes sinful men."[40]

At prayer we must be party people. We must candidly
confess that our world is overpopulated with elder brothers
who choose to remain outside. We must celebrate the reversals that occur in our own lives and the lives of our fellow
humans. Once we hear the disorientation-reorientation in
"dead/alive" and "lost/found" we must immediately add

[38] J. D. Crossan, *In Parables: The Challenge of the Historical Jesus* (New York:
Harper & Row, 1973) 74.

[39] Ibid., 73-74. See also E. Linnemann, *Jesus of the Parables* (New York: Harper
& Row, 1966) 80-81.

[40] C. H. Giblin, "Structural and Theological Considerations on Luke 15," *CBQ*
24 (1962) 25.

"make merry." Prayer is to be an experience whereby good news becomes contagious, urging on our message of joy and congratulations. To be such a partygoer is to confess our belief in a God who still performs miracles, especially for those who are seemingly insignificant (one sheep out of a hundred, one coin out of ten, one prodigal son versus an obedient one). Ours is a God who refuses to abide by our carefully enacted rules. Hence the transformation of a prodigal means prodigal celebration on the part all, not the pouting of supposedly correct and obedient children. To pray the thanksgiving or psalm of declarative praise is ultimately to prepare for the banquet which is the consummation of the kingdom (see Matt 8:11). Only partygoers are admitted.

Summary of the theology of the thanksgiving or the psalms of declarative praise[41]

(1) We are challenged to reject "new" as a dirty three-letter word. We are urged to admit a God of surprises.

(2) We are invited to imitate our God in the transformation of chaos into cosmos. We are called upon to effect surprises for others because we believe in a God of surprises.

(3) We are encouraged to see our gifts as gifts for others. It is these gifts which can counteract the inhumanity of our world and thus bring about reorientation.

(4) We are asked to observe the goodness of others and to label it "good, very good." Our God continues to surprise us in and through others.

(5) We are compelled to rediscover our sense of celebration. In Eucharist we are to share the burdens of others by sharing the bread and the wine. To celebrate Eucharist is to restore our God's capacity to give and effect surprises.

[41] Other psalms of declarative praise include the following: (a) individual: 31, 41, 92, 103, 107, 116, 138; (b) communal: 67.

Index of Biblical Passages

Index of Authors